For Jonathan — You're one of us; wha's like us!! --- So flaunt your Scottishness! With love Iain

June '97

SCOTTISH FIRSTS

INNOVATION AND ACHIEVEMENT

SCOTTISH FIRSTS

INNOVATION AND ACHIEVEMENT

Researched and written by Elspeth Wills, Edinburgh.
Designed by Gordon Rennie Graphic Design, Glasgow.
Printed by McCorquodale (Scotland) Ltd.

©
Published by
Scottish Development Agency
120 Bothwell Street
Glasgow G2 7JP
Tel: 041-248 2700

ADAM SMITH

CONTENTS

THE Scots in particular were possessed with that romantic speculative inventiveness crossed with the mentality of a chartered accountant.

CHARLES WILSON

Introduction

JAMES WATT

"You come of a race of men the very wind of whose name has swept to the ultimate seas."
Sir James Barrie: Rectorial Address to students of St Andrews University

Introduction

Joseph Black *(1728-1799).*
ack: National Galleries of Scotland, Edinburgh.

Warship: **HMS Hood,** built on the Clyde.
ack: University of Glasgow Archives.

What do radar, road surfaces and the rotary engine have in common, or finger printing, facsimile transmission and the fountain pen? What linked thirteen American Presidents, the Empress Eugenie and the composer Elgar? Where was the first milk bar, the first mechanics institute and the first mine to be lit by electricity?

The clue lies in a small country with five million inhabitants, a long and often turbulent history and a wild and rugged landscape: Scotland. From this small corner of the globe have come great scientists like James Clerk Maxwell and David Brewster, engineers of the calibre of Watt and Kelvin and doctors of the class of James Young Simpson and Sir Alexander Fleming. Scotland has over the centuries not only exported her innovations and technology but also her people, to explore, to work and to settle. Of the 73 Americans in the US Great Hall of Fame, no fewer than 25 had Scots blood in their veins. Large tracts of countries such as Canada, Australia and New Zealand were settled mainly by Scots as the placenames of Dunedin, Perth and Hamilton recall.

It is not just the Scotsman's pride in his homeland that has earned Scotland a place on the world map of innovation. Otherwise why did the Frenchman Voltaire comment "It is from Scotland that we receive rules of taste in all the arts", or the American, Thomas Jefferson claim that in the context of its scientific contribution "No place in the world can pretend to competition with Edinburgh", or the Welsh Prime Minister, Lloyd George complain "the Scots have only got one bad fault: there are too few of them". It is difficult, objectively, to measure the "greatness" of a nation. Such studies as have been undertaken from Francis Galton's "Hereditary Genius" to Havelock Ellis's "Study of Genius" have all turned to Scotland for their inspiration. More recently and more prosaically perhaps, a recent US Census Bureau study of the US descendants of emigrants from eight European countries showed that Americans of Scots descent had the best record of educational achievement, were best off financially and were most likely to be in employment. They were also the most likely to be married!

Why should such a small country nurture so many men and women whose ideas, actions and descendants shaped the world? There is no one simple answer. A part of the reason lies in the very poverty of parts of the country which in past centuries could not hope to sustain all its sons. The enterprising looked to the growing industrial towns of southern Scotland, to London, the eternal mecca of the young, and to the opportunities of the newer lands. It was after all the descendant of a Scot, the United States newspaper editor, Horace Greeley, who offered his adopted countrymen the immortal advice "Go West, Young Man".

A small country bounded on three sides by sea, Scotland has been a trading and exporting nation from earliest times. From medieval trading links with Norway and the Baltic, the Scots extended their trading empire to the sugar plantations of the Caribbean and the tobacco fields of the American South. In the 18th century, alongside the Glasgow "Tobacco Lords", grew up the "Nabobs", enterprising Scots who helped to develop the trade and administration of the Indian sub-continent. In the 19th century Scotland's industrial heartland provided the world with the products of its engineering workshops earning Glasgow the title of "Second City of the British Empire". Locomotives for South Africa, ships for Japan, floating docks for Java, all started life in Glasgow.

The Tobacco Lords, the Tolbooth, Glasgow.
ack: People's Palace Museum, Glasgow.

"THE QUEENS"
Queen Elizabeth on river and *inset* **Queen Mary**—fitting out.
ack: University of Glasgow Archives.

Queen Elizabeth II.

David Hume (1711-1776).
ack: National Galleries of Scotland, Edinburgh.

Scottish engineering not only produced the "Queens" but also attracted the world's royalty as its customers. Where else did the Tsar look when he wished a circular steam yacht, or the Maharajah Scindia of Gwalior when his fancy turned to summer palaces? Engineering still plays a crucial role today accounting for over half of Scotland's manufactured exports, the diversity of which extends to yashmaks to the Arabs and snowballs to the Eskimos.

This centuries-long tradition of trade has spun off other skeins, which have provided the threads of Scotland's innovative place in the world. Trading links have encouraged other links, cultural, social and academic. They helped to foster a cosmopolitan attitude, a readiness to exchange ideas and adopt new practices that has characterised much of Scottish thinking. These attitudes were encapsulated in the Scottish Enlightenment when for half a century Edinburgh was truly the "Athens of the North" and men like David Hume and Adam Smith rethought the world.

It was the practical philosophy of such men who stressed the need for logic and clear thinking that lay behind the achievements of the Scots scientists of the day. Men like Joseph Black, the physical chemist, John Hunter, the surgeon and James Hall, the geologist took up the message of empiricism and introduced the idea of experimental verification into their chosen disciplines. The number of Scots who have been awarded the title, "Father of" so many modern scientific disciplines, from electronics to brain surgery, is tribute to this way of thinking.

Calvinism also played its part in shaping Scotland's contribution to the world. Its emphasis on hard work, material values and education provided the impetus for many to achieve. Its stern precepts fuelled the moral fervour of the Scottish missionary-explorers and of the social and medical reformers. Its fundamentalism tied in with the philosophies of the emergent nations with their belief in freedom, democracy and the rights of man. Its teaching was enshrined in men like Andrew Carnegie, the son of a radical Dunfermline weaver, who rose to become one of America's greatest millionaires of all time. He gave his wealth

Sir Alexander Fleming *(1881-1955).*
ack: National Galleries of Scotland, Edinburgh.

Aberdeen University—King's College *(c. 1640).*
Reproduced with the permission of the University Court from a painting in Aberdeen University.

University of St Andrews—St Salvator's Quadrangle.
ack: University of St Andrews

James Watt *(1736-1819).*
ack: National Galleries of Scotland, Edinburgh.

Glasgow University from the south. *ack: University of Glasgow.*
Inset: **Edinburgh University**—part of the Old College looking across to the Castle.
ack: Information Services, University of Edinburgh.

back to the people in the shape of libraries, museums, scholarships, church organs and the International Court of Justice in the Hague. Calvinism may have had an even stronger correlation with invention! In the period from the Reformation until the turn of the 20th century, Scottish clergymen who at no time exceeded 0.1% of the population fathered more than an eighth of the great Scottish scientists.

It is in the development of education that lies one of the driving forces behind Scotland's innovative tradition. Scots have always put great store by education. As early as 1492 the Scottish Parliament passed an Act requiring the sons of burgesses to receive some form of elementary education; this was the first move towards compulsory education in Europe. By 1600, Scotland had four Universities. The rest of the UK had only two until well into the 19th century. While Oxford and Cambridge slumbered in their academic cloisters, constrained by tradition and religious convention, the Scottish Universities were rising to the forefront of the technologies that shaped the Industrial Revolution. Their emphasis shifted early from the rigours of a classical education to the new challenge of engineering and the increasing need for specialisation within science. James Watt was a technician at Glasgow University when he was asked to repair the Newcomen engine that set him dreaming of perfection. The links between the academic and the business worlds were close and productive. Joseph Black found time from his fundamental study of heat to improve the manufacture of writing paper and to develop means of extracting alginic acid from seaweed, an industry that thrives in Scotland to this day. Kelvin was a successful businessman as well as a scientist and engineer of international repute. He, like many Scots, combined the attitudes of thinker and doer.

This book sets out to describe the achievements of some of the great men that this small corner of the world produced—from major advances in medical science to the invention of everyday objects like the bicycle and the raincoat. Some will be the retelling of familiar stories, of the first practical demonstration of television and of the first telephone call, of the first baby to be born under anaesthesia and of the discovery of penicillin. Some will be less familiar such as the Dundee eccentric who produced continuous electric light 35 years before Swan or Edison, or the fertile mind of Robert Thomson which gave us the fountain pen and the pneumatic tyre as well as the portable steam crane and the road steamer. Most examples will relate to past achievements not because the Scots have rested on their laurels but because the individual inventor has now been caught up in the corporate wheel of invention and is more difficult to pinpoint.

Most important of all, only time will separate the breakthroughs of the future from the bright ideas of today.

Scottish Men of Science

JAMES CLERK MAXWELL

"To few men in the world has such an experience been vouchsafed."
Albert Einstein

Scottish Men of Science

So wrote Albert Einstein on the work of a shy, retiring Scotsman, James Clerk Maxwell, who laid down the principles of modern electronics. Einstein himself could only claim admiration for the Scottish scientific achievement but Ambrose Fleming, the inventor of the diode, Ernest Rutherford who split the atom and gave birth to nuclear physics, J J Thomson who unravelled the mysteries of the electron and Isaac Newton himself all claimed Scottish blood in their veins. Scots can look nearer home for their contribution to scientific progress in areas as diverse as the theory of heat, determination of the solar parallax and the origins of the world itself.

Why did such a small and relatively poor country produce so many men of science? It is said that the Scots character combines the mixture of tenacity, idealism and canny good sense that form the bedrock of scientific achievement. Is it coincidental that so many of Scotland's distinguished scientists, men like David Brewster and Thomas Graham, were destined, by their fathers, for the ministry? The Scottish educational tradition with its emphasis on education for all and on breadth of grounding certainly played its part.

Scottish scientists bear no resemblance to the caricature boffin with a one-track mind and his head in the clouds. At his Golden Wedding, Sir James Dewar played the fiddle that he had made himself as a child. Dr James Gregory was the lion of Edinburgh literary circles and was called upon whenever the public authorities required the civic dignity of a Latin inscription. Their feet were also firmly on the ground. Many were aware of the practical applications of their discoveries and sought to develop them. David Brewster devoted much time and anxiety to marketing his kaleidoscope. James Hutton only took up geology after a highly successful career as a chemical manufacturer.

Part of the reason behind the degree of scientific achievement, especially in the 18th and early 19th centuries, was the smallness and closeness of the scientific community. This allowed for a free flow of ideas and a cross-fertilisation between different scientific disciplines. Joseph Black's work on heat provided inspiration for James Watt in his perfection of the steam engine. When Watt moved south he became a member of the Lunar Society, a group of scientists who met during the full moon so that travelling home would be easier. A fellow member was Erasmus Darwin, grandfather of Charles who collaborated with the Scot Alfred Russell Wallace in the publication of the Theory of Evolution, and became a close personal friend of the Scots geologist Charles Lyell. Lyell devoted much of his life to publicising the work of fellow geologist, James Hutton. It was owing to Hutton's indisposition that the first part of his classic paper on the "Theory of the Earth" was read to the Royal Society of Edinburgh by none other than Joseph Black. And so it comes full circle.

The first major contribution to science from Scotland came, however, not from the Universities but from the aristocracy. Until recently when the calculator took the place of its 17th century equivalent, every schoolboy loved to hate him.

John Napier (1550-1617)

Napier, the 8th Laird of Merchiston, was born into the Scottish aristocracy. His family seat now forms the focal point of Napier College, Edinburgh's college of advanced technology.

Napier lived in stirring times when Scotland was being torn apart by the religious upheaval of the Reformation. He was a staunch Protestant and in 1593 published a bitterly anti-Catholic attack on the Revelation of St John. He directed his inventive mind to designing several instruments of war to meet the threat of an invasion from the Spanish. Fortunately, the threat did not materialise. His contraptions of war included the forerunner of the armoured tank, a primitive submarine, a "burning mirror" constructed with lenses to use as a fire raising weapon, and artillery that could destroy life within a mile's radius.

Fortunately it is for his mathematical, rather than his military achievements, that Napier has gone down in history. He devised an early form of calculating machine known as "Napier's bones" and he put the point into the decimal fraction.

In 1594 it occurred to him that all numbers could be expressed in exponential form. Once this had been achieved, multiplication could be undertaken simply by adding the exponents and division by subtracting them. He devoted the next twenty years to working out complex formulae for obtaining exponential expressions of various numbers, with particular emphasis on the exponential forms of the trigonometric functions which were extensively used in astronomical calculations. The process he devised, of computing the exponential expressions, led him to call them proportionate numbers or logarithms. It may be that this mammoth task of twenty years was undertaken in his search for the number of the Beast of the Apocalypse: its practical results had a much wider impact.

In 1614, he at last published the fruits of his labours which were immediately seized upon with delight by fellow mathematicians and astronomers. They

John Napier (1550-1617).
ack: National Galleries of Scotland, Edinburgh.

relieved scientists of a great part of the drudgery of non-creative calculations. It is difficult now to imagine the scale of their impact which cannot have been dissimilar to the impact of computers in the 20th century.

The 17th century also saw the emergence of a name that was to be recorded in the annals of science for many generations.

The Gregory Family

The Gregory family, whose members played a pre-eminent role in Scottish scientific life from the 17th to the 19th century, is remarkable not only for the quality but also for the sheer quantity of achievement. From the marriage of one Janet Anderson to an Aberdeenshire parish minister, John Gregorie, there ensued no less than sixteen professors. Indeed Francis Galton in his classic, "Hereditary Genius", cites the family as an example of the inheritance of scientific gifts. Perhaps nature did help a little to lessen the odds; one early Gregory had twenty nine children!

Their talents probably stemmed from the maternal side of the family. Janet Anderson's father was nicknamed "Davie do a' thing" because of his many practical skills; a relative was Professor of Mathematics at Paris University and Janet, herself a distinguished mathematician, was responsible for the education of her son James.

Before the age of 24, James Gregory (1638-75) proposed the idea of the reflecting telescope. It was only because he could not find a glassmaker competent to handle the complexity of his design that he failed to produce a practical instrument. This was left for Newton to achieve in 1668. Gregory also suggested the determination of the solar parallax by reference to the transition of Venus and Mercury. Until the 19th century this method was used to determine the distance of the sun. As a mathematician, Gregory made a number of significant contributions with his general statement of the binomial theorem and his introduction into the language of algebra of the term "convergent series". He anticipated Newton and Leibnitz in many aspects of calculus and even solved Zeno's paradox of Achilles and the tortoise which had been teasing the minds of mathematicians for many centuries. After spending several years in Padua, Gregory returned to his native Scotland to take up the Chair of Mathematics at St Andrews University. This was not perhaps the most onerous of tasks as its duties consisted of two lectures a week and the responsibility for answering any mathematical questions that might be put to the incumbent. He left St Andrews in 1674 to take up a Chair at Edinburgh University, somewhat in disgrace with the authorities because of his advanced views. He was one of the first people to adopt the new physics of Newton. His reign at Edinburgh was to be short lived. One evening while showing some students the satellites of Jupiter he was struck blind and died a few days later.

The authorities were prepared to wait. After eight years without an appointment to the Chair they gave it to James' nephew, David Gregory, who at the age of twenty-two had not yet even completed his degree. He continued very much in his uncle's footsteps being the first person to propose the achromatic telescope and to observe that by inverting the curve made by a chain, fixed at both ends, the legitimate form of an arch is arrived at. His main contribution to science, however, lay not so much in his own original work but in his influence as proponent, supporter and populariser of Newtonian physics both in Edinburgh and later at Oxford. He was a close friend of Newton and wrote the first textbook based on gravitational principles.

A 19th century music hall ballad celebrates the fame of one of the later members of the family, Professor James Gregory (1753-1821).

"If in doubt lead with trumps is counsel so old
As never to fail with the game in a fixture
And medical men in their doubt I am told
Are safe when they lead with Gregory's mixture."

Gregory's mixture was the mainstay of the Victorian nursery as a cure for stomach ache. His compound of rhubarb, magnesia and ginger was in its day the most widely prescribed remedy in the pharmacopoeia. He was a physician of the "vigorous" school: disease according to his view was to be attacked by a combination of free blood letting, the cold effusion, frequent purging and blistering and the use of tartar emetic. Gregory was also a literary figure in Edinburgh society as a Latin scholar and translator of poetry. His directness of approach in poetic criticism as well as in medicine led Robert Burns to comment "I believe in the iron justice of Dr Gregory, but like the devil, I believe and tremble".

The last of the Professorial Gregorys, William Gregory (1803-58) adopted his preferred discipline of chemistry, early in life. His later ill health was attributed to his having breathed noxious fumes as a child. A friend of the great German chemist Liebig, Gregory perfected the preparation of several chemical compounds including hydrochloric acid, chloroform and morphia. One can also argue, somewhat tongue in cheek, that Gregory was the father of the Middle East

James Gregory (1638-1675).
ack: National Galleries of Scotland, Edinburgh.

Professor James Gregory (1753-1821).
ack: National Galleries of Scotland, Edinburgh.

Scottish Men of Science

Robert Brown (1773-1858).
ack: National Galleries of Scotland, Edinburgh.

Joseph Black (1728-1799).
From John Kay's Original Portraits and Etchings,
ack: Mitchell Library, Glasgow.

oil industry as he was the first person to extract a usable product, in this case, paraffin, from Persian naphtha. Having succeeded in the academic challenge of extracting something from the piece of naphtha, Gregory did not investigate further and left the title of "Father of the Oil Industry" to be taken up by fellow Scot, James Young.

Scotland's contribution to scientific progress covered all the major disciplines: physics, mathematics, chemistry, geology and the life sciences. The influence, however, that the workers in these fields have achieved over time crosses the boundaries of specific disciplines. The work of the Edinburgh chemist George Beilby (1850-1924) on the thin layer of molecules that forms on polished materials has taken on new significance in research into the latest generation of semiconductors. In the course of his plant research, an Edinburgh botanist was to lay down some of the first developments in cell theory and in atomism.

Robert Brown (1773-1858)

The son of an Anglican clergyman from Montrose, Brown spent his early years as a medical man in the army and his spare time pursuing his hobby of botany. In the latter capacity he attracted the attention of Sir Joseph Banks. It was due to his influence that Brown gained a position as naturalist on an expedition to the still largely unexplored continent of Australia. The ships returned with over 4000 specimens, a larger number than had been brought back by all previous expeditions to Australia put together.

As a consequence of his work in classifying the collection, Brown was appointed Librarian to the Linnaean Society as well as acting as librarian in a personal capacity to Banks who on his death bequeathed his house, his library and his botanical collections to him.

Brown's lasting reputation, however, is due to two major discoveries. Like other researchers before him, Brown was aware of a small body within the cells of a plant that composed the plant tissue. Unlike his predecessors, however, Brown recognised this as a regular feature of cells and in 1831 named it nucleus after the Latin "little nut", the name it has borne ever since. His discovery led to the development a decade later of cell theory by Virchov and the Scottish scientist, John Goodsir, who stressed that the cell is the starting point for all plant and animal life.

Brown's other major discovery bears his own name and has had significant repercussions outside the field of science in which he was working—Brownian motion. This resulted from a routine investigation of plant pollen in 1827. One day as Brown was viewing a suspension of pollen under a microscope, he noted that the individual grains were moving about irregularly. Brown at first attributed this to hidden "life" within the pollen but when he repeated the same experiments with grains of dyestuff he found the same effect. This was the first evidence for atomism that was based on observation rather than deduction. As with the nucleus, later Scots, notably James Clerk Maxwell in his kinetic theory of gases, Thomas Graham in his work on colloids and William Ramsay, in his explanation of the energy that caused the motion, all helped to unravel the mystery.

In physics, Scottish scientists have made a major contribution to man's knowledge of heat, both hot and cold. Joseph Black laid down some of the fundamental principles of the behaviour of heat.

Joseph Black (1728-1799)

Son of a Scottish wine merchant in Bordeaux, Black returned to his native land to receive his education. He studied medicine at Glasgow and Edinburgh Universities where he was later to hold Professorial chairs. His interest as a student in kidney stones led him to study other minerals that had similar properties. His thesis for his medical degree, published in 1756, proved to be a classic of chemistry. In it he showed that the compound calcium carbonate could be converted to calcium oxide on strong heating, giving off a gas which could recombine with calcium oxide to form calcium carbonate again. Black called the gas "fixed air" because it could be fixed into solid form again: it is better known as carbon dioxide. Given that calcium oxide could be converted to calcium carbonate simply by exposure to the air it followed that carbon dioxide was a normal constituent of the atmosphere.

While studying the behaviour of carbon dioxide, Black observed that even after removing the carbon dioxide from a closed container in which a candle had been burnt the remaining air would not support a flame. Black turned this problem over to his young assistant, Daniel Rutherford who, as well as becoming an eminent scientist in his own right, was also the uncle of Sir Walter Scott! From working on this problem, Rutherford discovered that nitrogen was an independent constituent of air which does not support combustion. Joseph Priestley, however, beat him to publication by several months.

About 1760 Black's interests turned to the phenomenon of heat. He was the first person to recognise that the quantity of heat is not the same thing as its intensity: it was the latter only that was measured as temperature. He found, for example, that when ice was heated it slowly melted but did not change in temperature. Ice absorbed a quantity of "latent heat" on melting, increasing the amount of heat it contained but not the intensity.

The heat taken up by water in boiling was a clue to the far greater energy content of steam at the boiling point temperature as compared with an equal weight of liquid water at the same temperature. This point and the work of Black in general was known to James Watt who utilised it in his development of steam power.

Black also discovered what is now known as specific heat. He showed that when equal weights of two different substances are brought together and are allowed to come to temperature equilibrium, the final temperature is not necessarily at the midway point. Black himself had some difficulties in coming to terms with his discoveries as like all scientists of the time he believed that heat was an imponderable fluid, as was light and electricity. It was only when the kinetic theory of heat was developed by James Clerk Maxwell, that Black's experiments fell neatly into place.

Like many scientists Black's interests were wide ranging and embraced the practical as well as the theoretical. He was, for example, one of the first people to grasp the potential of hydrogen for balloons and he introduced the manufacture of writing paper by the chemical bleaching of rags thus significantly reducing the price of paper, which had previously been made from unprinted linen.

It was another Scottish scientist who finally laid to rest the idea that heat was a kind of fluid. His crowning achievement was even greater.

James Clerk Maxwell *(1831-1879)*

How Maxwell's school mates must have lived to rue the day that they nicknamed one of the world's greatest scientists "dafty", as later did both Aberdeen and Edinburgh University rue rejecting him for Professorial chairs.

The son of a Dumfriesshire landowner, Maxwell was brought up in Edinburgh where his modest personality and country ways made him an easy target for the taunts of his fellow schoolboys. He was even as a child more at home in the company of august professors. His first paper on geometry was read to the Royal Society of Edinburgh when he had only just turned fifteen. He studied mathematics at Cambridge where he had a brilliant career. It is said that when he finished one examination in record time, he amused himself by translating the examination paper into Latin. He then went on to teach first at Aberdeen and then at Kings College, London before becoming the first holder of the Cavendish Chair of Physics at Cambridge. There he helped to set up the world famous Cavendish laboratory and to recruit its first staff. A retiring person who only fully came to life when deep in discussion of some mathematical or philosophical point, Maxwell was at his happiest working and experimenting in the attic of his Dumfriesshire home.

It was in research of the most fundamental and original nature that Maxwell's true genius lay, a genius which was only fully recognised in the 20th century. He is now generally regarded as second only to Newton and Einstein in the history of science.

How did this shy man come to overthrow the existing model of the physical world? His first area of research was devoted to the study of the behaviour of gases. By employing rigorous statistical method Maxwell developed the kinetic theory of gases, demonstrating that the particles within a gas moved constantly and at random and working out the equation to identify the "average" velocity of a gas. His work finally laid to rest the established belief of heat as a kind of fluid. He redirected scientific thinking away from the determinism of classical physics towards the idea of probability underlying so much of modern physics. He founded the science of statistical mechanics and originated the concepts of cybernetics.

He then moved on to what was to be his greatest contribution to modern science. He took the ideas of Michael Faraday on electricity and subjected them to the most rigorous mathematical examination. He proved beyond any doubt the indissoluble link between electricity and magnetism and gave the world a new word and a new theory "electromagnetism". Using his equation he showed that the oscillation of an electric charge would produce an electromagnetic field radiating from its source at a constant velocity. He worked out the velocity which was roughly the velocity of light and suggested that light was a kind of electromagnetic radiation. From Maxwell's electromagnetic spectrum came the long and short waves of radio and radar and the ultra-short waves of X-rays. Without Maxwell's fundamental leap in the dark, much of today's electronics revolution might not have happened.

Another of Maxwell's lifelong interests was in optics. He demonstrated that every colour can be matched by a combination of three suitably chosen spectral colours and developed the theory of colour in relation to colour blindness. He took the world's first colour photograph which he exhibited to a meeting of the Royal Institution in 1861. The subject was a tartan ribbon bow taken against a black, velvet background. He had the ribbon photographed three times using colour filters consisting of red, green and blue bottles of liquid which were placed between the camera and the subject. Glass positives from the collodion

James Clerk Maxwell *(1831-1879)*.
James Clerk Maxwell, Mrs Maxwell and dog.
ack: University of Cambridge, Cavendish Laboratory.

negatives were then projected on a screen by three separate lanterns, each lantern being fitted with a filter to correspond with its transparency.

Maxwell did not live to see the fruits of his quiet revolution. Nearly a century was to pass before the extent of his genius was generally acknowledged; although long before then men like Marconi and Rontgen were verifying his principles through their practice.

Sir James Dewar (1847-1932)
ack: National Galleries of Scotland, Edinburgh.

Sir James Dewar's interests lay at the other end of the temperature scale. In pursuit of the very cold, he gave to the world a means of keeping things hot, the vacuum flask.

Sir James Dewar (1847-1932)

This eminent scientist and inventor of the Dewar or Thermos flask was born in the village of Kincardine on Forth, the son of the chief innkeeper of the village. As a child, Dewar suffered from rheumatic fever, a result of falling through the ice. During his long convalescence he became friendly with the local joiner who taught him how to make fiddles. This early training laid the basis for Dewar's later reputation for manipulative skills.

He attended Edinburgh University for several years serving as a laboratory assistant to Professor J D Forbes, the noted glaciologist and the first man to polarise heat, Lyon Playfair and Alexander Crum Brown who is known for his formulation of the structure of organic compounds. These three men did much to shape Dewar's future interests.

In 1867, Dewar published his first scientific paper in which he described a sort of "lazy tong" method of representing carbon compounds including seven different ways to represent benzene. This paper brought him to the attention of Kekule the noted chemist with whom he spent a summer in Delft. Kekule has gone down in scientific history as the deviser of the formula to represent benzene; he selected one of Dewar's seven possible examples.

After a few years as a lecturer in the Royal Veterinary College in Edinburgh, Dewar was appointed to the Jacksonian Chair of Natural Experimental Philosophy at Cambridge. Although he held this post until his death, the somewhat conservative and academic atmosphere of Cambridge at the time did not suit him. His temperament was very much that of the blunt outspoken Scot and the practical, experimental scientist. In 1877, he additionally became Fullerian Professor at the Royal Institution in London, in whose laboratories he carried out most of his notable work.

It was the discovery by a French and a Swiss chemist of the possibility of liquefying oxygen and hydrogen that turned Dewar's interest from high temperature to low temperature physics. It was in relation to his work on the liquefaction of gases that he designed in 1892 the vacuum flask. This consisted of a double lined vessel with a vacuum between the two layers. In his work over the previous 20 years he had used the principle of vacuum insulation but his current researches demanded the use of a vessel which would hold the liquid gases, keep them cold and prevent the formation of frost. Dewar's original flasks were unsilvered but he later added a drop of mercury which condensed to form a mirror at liquid air temperatures.

He improved his design further in 1904 by the use of a minute amount of charcoal in the vacuum which acted as an absorbent of any remaining gases. Until then the vessel had to be made of glass which rendered it relatively fragile, due to the fact that metal gives off a quantity of gas when heated. The insertion of charcoal, however, meant that the gas could be absorbed, and thus made feasible the use of a metal container as the outer layer of the flask.

The early flasks were extremely fragile and required careful handling. It was only when Dewar met a German glassblowing expert, Reinhold Burger, that the first successful flask was made. Commercial production of Dewar's flask began in 1898. Initially the flask was intended for use only in scientific laboratories. Although Dewar was aware of the flask's ability to keep liquids hot as well as cold, he showed no interest in the potential commercial application of his invention and did not take out any patents on the device. It was left to Burger to put the Thermos flask in every picnic basket!

Dewar continued with his scientific research happy to let others realise the commercial potential of his flask. The First World War brought a halt to his cryogenic research due to lack of resources and in his final years he turned to research into thin films such as soap bubbles.

The chemists, on the other hand, were more interested in heat as a mechanism for exploring the make-up of the elements. It was boiling argon that gave Sir William Ramsay the key to the other rare constituents of air.

Sir William Ramsay (1852-1916)

The Glaswegian born Ramsay could be described as an all rounder. As a child he was interested in music and languages before his interests swung towards mathematics and science. He was also a keen athlete. He even showed a talent for glassblowing and in later life made most of his own scientific glassware. After studying in Tubingen, in Germany from where he obtained his PhD in 1873, he became Professor of Chemistry first at Bristol and then at University College, London.

A problem that had puzzled scientists for some time was the evidence that suggested that there might be a trace of some gas in air that was heavier than nitrogen, and that did not combine with oxygen. Using a spectroscope, Ramsay identified a new gas in air that made up about one per cent of the atmosphere. Because the new gas was inert and would not combine with any other element, Ramsay and his colleague Rayleigh christened it argon, after the Greek word for inert. Various pointers suggested to Ramsay that the gas was not unique but belonged to a family of gases sharing the same characteristics.

In 1895, he began his search for the other members of the family—helium, neon, krypton and xenon. His patient and methodical search yielded results. Having searched the other minerals in vain, Ramsay and his assistant tried fractionating argon, after obtaining it from liquid air. After months of preparing fifteen litres of argon they liquefied it and allowed it to boil. The first fraction contained a new, light gas which they called neon; the last fractions contained two heavy gases which they touchingly called krypton and xenon after the Greek words for hidden and stranger.

Ramsay's discovery of the other member of the family, helium, in uranium ores gave him an interest in radioactivity. In 1903, working with Frederick Soddy, he was able to show that helium was continually produced by naturally radioactive products. When Dorn finally found the missing member of the family, radon, it was Ramsay who weighed a tiny quantity of the substance and determined its atomic weight.

He was knighted in 1902 and received the Nobel Prize for Chemistry in 1904 for his work on the inert gases.

In the Scottish contribution to scientific achievement chemistry also blends closely into medicine. William Cullen lectured in both subjects. Although he held the Chair of the Institutes of Medicine at Edinburgh University, his most lasting contribution, the artificial congelation of ice on which the principles of the refrigerator are based, lies very definitely in the sphere of physical science. Kidney machines are regarded as a lifesaver of modern medicine: the principle behind them, dialysis, was evolved by a Glasgow chemist.

Thomas Graham (1805-1869)

The son of a Glasgow merchant, Graham was the oldest of a family of seven. His father wanted him to become a minister after he graduated, but Graham had other ideas. He spent the next ten years studying at Edinburgh University under men like Professor Leslie, whose studies in radiation were celebrated in Leslie's cube. It was during this period that Graham earned his first payment for literary work: he spent his earnings of £6 on presents for his mother to whom he was devoted.

Realising the need to earn a living, Graham returned to Glasgow and became firstly lecturer in chemistry at the Glasgow Mechanics Institute and in 1830 Professor of Chemistry at the Andersonian Institution. He moved to London in 1837 to take up the Chair of Chemistry at the recently founded, University College. In 1855 he succeeded Sir John Herschel as Master of the Royal Mint.

Graham's fundamental work in chemistry was far in advance of his contemporaries and was also characterised by its originality and simplicity. Before 1840 he proved that phosphoric acid forms several different compounds with water and he even put forward the bold theory that all elements may be no more than different forms of one primordial element. He formulated the law of

Sir William Ramsay (1852-1916).
ack: Chemistry Department, University of Glasgow.

Thomas Graham (1805-69).
ack: Strathclyde University Archives, Glasgow.

the diffusion of gases that is still known as Graham's Law and in association with this research, developed the Graham tube, a simple device consisting of a glass tube with a plug of plaster of Paris at one end. His studies of the passage of gases through small openings and through films greatly extended knowledge of the motion of molecules. He discovered the principle of atmolysis, or the separation of gases. He is best known, however, as the "Father of Colloid Science"; he earned this title through his study of the manner in which liquids permeate membranes, which he named dialysis. He called substances which have high diffusibility, crystalloids, and substances which have low diffusibility, colloids.

Graham also took an active part in public and professional affairs. He served on several Government Committees including those to investigate the purity of London's water supply and the efficacy of the ventilation of the new Houses of Parliament. He acted as Vice-President and Reporter to the jury of the chemical and pharmaceutical section of the Great Exhibition of 1851. He was the first President of the Chemical Society when it was founded in 1840 and also the first President of the Cavendish Society. He was also twice Vice-President of the Royal Society.

Oxford honoured him with a degree and his international reputation was recognised by honorary membership of many Academies of Science, including Berlin, Munich, Turin and Washington.

In more recent times the disciplines of chemistry and medicine have merged to form the specialism of biochemistry. Here too, a Scot played a fundamental role in man's knowledge of the workings of his body.

Sir Alexander Robertus Todd (1907-)

Todd was born in Glasgow where he obtained his first degree before going on to study at Frankfurt and Oxford. As a lecturer at Edinburgh University, he began his investigation of thiamine (Vitamin B). He continued this research at the Lister Institute for Preventative Medicine, elucidating the structure and synthesis of the vitamin. The next substance to attract his scientific attention was cannabis, whose active principle he was able to isolate from the resin.

In 1944, he was appointed Professor of Organic Chemistry at Cambridge. His specialism was the study of the chemistry of the nucleic acids, DNA and RNA. He synthesised all the naturally-occurring nucleotide components of the nucleic acids and in doing so, provided experimental proof of Levene's deduction that the structures of the nucleotides produced compounds that were identical with those obtained from nucleic acids.

Todd continued his work on synthesising the nucleotides at Cambridge from 1944. He synthesised the compounds adenosine diphosphate and adenosine triphosphate which are of crucial significance in the handling of energy by the body. His work cleared the path for Watson and Crick and the discovery of DNA.

Todd was awarded the Nobel Prize for Chemistry in 1957 and was created a Baron in 1962.

Perhaps it is partly because Scotland is built on some of the world's oldest rock that the contribution to geology has been so fundamental!

The Hammer of The Scots

It was a combination of three Scots geologists who turned man's thinking about the earth and its origins on its axis.

The first of these was **James Hutton** (1726-1797), Edinburgh born and bred. Geology was Hutton's third career. He originally trained as a doctor but never practised. He then set up a plant manufacturing ammonium chloride; with James Davie he was the first to manufacture sal ammoniac by the sublimation of soot and to pioneer the production of sal volatile, the standby of every 19th century lady.

Encouraged by his close friend, the chemist Joseph Black, Hutton became increasingly interested in geology and in 1786, he sold his successful business to devote himself entirely to study. Geology before Hutton did not really exist as a discipline. There had been a number of sporadic discoveries but no one had put forward any general theory of the earth's development. In this scientists were constrained by the prevailing religious view of the creation of the Universe six thousand years ago as laid down in the Book of Genesis.

Hutton's studies convinced him that there had been a slow evolution of the earth's surface. Some rocks were laid down as sediment and compressed, others were formed of molten material thrust up from the interior of the earth by volcanic action and others were worn down by the action of wind and water. The innovative element in Hutton's careful argument was the idea that the forces now slowly operating to effect change in the earth's surface had been operating in the past at the same rate and in the same way. This was to become known as the "gradualist" or "uniformitarian" theory of the earth's formation.

He published his views in 1785 in a work entitled "The Theory of the Earth" in which incidentally he also put forward the modern theory of rainfall. The book met with considerable opposition especially in religious quarters. The widespread

Sir Alexander Todd (1907—).
Now Lord Todd of Trumpington here seen as Chancellor of the University of Strathclyde, October 1966.
ack: Strathclyde University Archives, Glasgow.

James Hutton (1726-1797).
ack: National Galleries of Scotland, Edinburgh.

adoption of Huttonian theory had to wait for the evangelising zeal of another Scottish geologist, Sir Charles Lyell.

Linking Hutton and Lyell was the work of **Sir James Hall** *(1761-1832)*. Hall, born in Haddington, was a Baronet and amateur geologist who was for a time a fellow student of Napoleon at the University of Brienne. Hall was a fervent admirer of Huttonian theory and decided to put it to practical test. A visit to a glass factory provided him with the inspiration. There he observed that when molten glass was cooled very slowly it became opaque and crystalline. He therefore had rock melted in a furnace and discovered that if the rock was cooled quickly it would form a glassy solid but if it was cooled slowly it would form a crystalline solid. He also demonstrated that if limestone was heated in a closed vessel it would not decompose but would melt and cool again to marble. Whereas time has christened Hutton the "Father of Geology" Hall may be regarded as the "Father of Experimental Geology" and indeed of Geochemistry. Hall proved Hutton's theory by exposing it to the application of laboratory techniques.

Surprisingly perhaps, Hutton disapproved of Hall's endeavours. He believed that one could not study vast planetary change by recourse to small laboratory experiments. Respecting his views, Hall did not publish his results until after Hutton's death.

About the time of Hall's death, **Charles Lyell** *(1797-1875)* published his three volume "Principles of Geology", the work that established Huttonian theory as the basis of geology. The work went into twelve editions in Lyell's lifetime. It was while Lyell, who was Angus born and bred, was a student at Oxford that his interest in geology developed. His own investigations on trips to the Continent made him think increasingly along gradualist lines. When he finally encountered Hutton's book, he realised that it paralleled his own thinking and vowed to give their joint views wider currency.

Although he was the first to name a number of geological eras including the Eocene and Pliocene, Lyell did not make any fundamental new contribution to geology: his achievement was in gaining widespread acceptance for the gradualist theory. Lyell's work inevitably led him into controversy with the more conventional scientists of his day and with prevailing religious opinion. One of his earliest converts was the young Darwin with whom he became very friendly. In his turn, when Darwin's theory of evolution was first proposed, Lyell was one of its earliest adherents. Indeed he himself went, albeit cautiously, into an area where Darwin at the time feared to tread by exploring in his book "The Antiquity of Man", published in 1863, the evolution of man. Although ultimate credit must go to Darwin as the father of evolution, another Scot, Alfred Russell Wallace developed the theory of natural selection independently and the theory was indeed launched in a paper he and Darwin prepared jointly.

Lyell was knighted for his work in 1848 and created a Baronet in 1864. Despite his somewhat controversial scientific views he was buried in Westminster Abbey alongside his friend Darwin.

Finally, there was a Scot who did have his head in the clouds, but clouds of great significance to nuclear physics.

Charles Thomson Rees Wilson *(1869-1959)*

Charles Wilson was born at Glencorse on the outskirts of Edinburgh, the son of a flourishing sheep farmer. When his father died in 1873, the family moved to Manchester. Wilson's love of clouds which he had inherited from the wide open landscapes of his earliest childhood was to lead him in quite unexpected directions.

He had a brilliant career at Cambridge and won the scholarship named after James Clerk Maxwell, a man with whom he had a lot in common. While working in J J Thomson's laboratory, Wilson tried to replicate on a small scale the cloud effects he had observed on the top of Ben Nevis, Scotland's highest mountain. He observed from his experiments that the droplets that went to form a cloud would only form in air with dust particles in it. In the absence of dust, Wilson postulated that clouds must form by condensing about ions in the air. The electrical charge of these ions could serve as nuclei whereas ordinary neutral molecules could not. When Wilson learned of the discovery of X-rays and of radioactivity, he was able to prove his theory by showing that ion formation as a result of those radiations could bring about more intensive cloud formation in the absence of dust.

Over a decade of experimentation, Wilson found not only that water droplets formed about the ions produced by energetic radiation and by speeding particles but that the radiation and particles left a track of such ions as they moved. This track became visible in the form of water droplets that appeared when the chamber that Wilson had devised for his experiments was expanded. By 1911, the Wilson cloud chamber was perfected and offered a way of making the events of the subatomic world visible to the human eye. The stimulation which Wilson's cloud chamber gave to atomic physics cannot be overestimated: a picture which had previously taken researchers years, painfully and partially to fit together, could now be seen in striking detail as a whole. In the course of his research Wilson became the first man to undertake a deliberate investigation of cosmic

Sir Charles Lyell *(1797-1875)*.

ack: National Galleries of Scotland, Edinburgh.

Sir James Hall *(1761-1832)*
ack: National Galleries of Scotland, Edinburgh.

Charles T R Wilson *(1869-1959)*.
ack: Glasgow Herald and Evening Times.

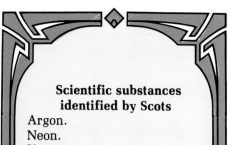

Scientific substances identified by Scots

Argon.
Neon.
Krypton.
Xenon.
Helium.
Carbon dioxide.
Isotropic diamonds.
Osmium.
Iridium.
Nitrogen.
Pyridene.
Picolene.
Lutidene.
Collidene.
Anthracene.
Thyroxine.
Coniine.
Protactinium.
Sodium pyrophosphate.
Phosgene.
Liquid oxygen.
Cinchonine.
Liquid nitrogen.
Dewar benzene.
Penicillin.
Lysozyme.
Liquid hydrogen.
Pure chloroform.
Morphine hydrochloride.
Morphine.
Strontium.
Interferon.
Lithopone.
The nitroprussides.

Units of measurement named by or after Scots

The degree Kelvin.
The Watt.
The therm.
The degree Rankine.
The Henry.
The horse power.

Scottish scientists' names live on

The Beilby layer
Crum Brown's rule
The Purdie reaction
Brownian movement
Brewster's Law
Graham's Law
The Ivory theory
Maxwell's Demon
Newland's Law
The Rankine cycle
The Gordon-Rankine formula.

radiation. Another lifelong interest was in thunderstorms, significantly increasing man's understanding of this phenomenon.

In 1927, Wilson was awarded the Nobel Prize in Physics but despite the wealth of international honours and tributes to his work—Ernest Rutherford described the cloud chamber as "the most original piece of apparatus in the whole history of science"—Wilson remained his modest, unassuming self. He combined determination and patience with an intuitive creativity. His cloud chamber was a model of elegance and simplicity and these characteristics held true for all his teaching and research.

Wilson never lost the love of his native Scotland. He holidayed each year in the Highlands or the Isle of Arran and some of his experimental work was undertaken in a railway tunnel outside Peebles. When he retired he came back to live in a small village outside Edinburgh where he roamed the hills and watched the clouds that had provided such a wealth of inspiration.

Scientific discoveries

The constitution of carbohydrate molecules: **Sir James Irvine.** *1877-1953.*
The physical chemistry of polymerisation: **Sir Harry Melville.** *b. 1908.*
The law of equipartition of kinetic energy among molecules of a gas: **John Waterston.** *1811-84.*
The doctrine of available energy: **Lord Kelvin.** *1824-1907.*
The theory of combustion: **Joseph Black.** *1728-99.*
The theory of electrical oscillations: **Lord Kelvin.** *1824-1907.*
Correlation of molecular structure with pharmacological effect: **Alexander Crum Brown.** *1838-1922.*
The idea of a gas as distinct from air: **Joseph Black.** *1728-99.*
The demonstration that DNA is an uninterrupted single molecule: **D. Callan.** *1958.*
The proof that mammals can lay eggs: **William Hay Caldwell.**
The theory of carbon as quadrivalent and able to form linkages with other atoms: **Archibald Couper.** *1831-92.*
Determination of the atomic weight of plutonium: **William Dittmar.** *1833-92.*
Demonstration that water reaches a maximum density at 4-6°C: **John Hope.** *1725-86.*
Fluorescence in chlorophyll: **Sir David Brewster.** *1781-1868.*
The carbon double bond in ethylene: **Alexander Crum Brown.** *1838-1922.*
Determination of the mean level of the sea: **James Jardine.** *1776-1858.*
The principle of the heat pump: **Lord Kelvin.** *1824-1907.*
The development of the wave theory of light: **Lord Kelvin.** *1824-1907.*
The development of molecular dynamics: **Lord Kelvin.** *1824-1907.*
The development of the second law of thermodynamics: **Lord Kelvin.** *1824-1907.*
The lowering of the freezing point of water by pressure: **James Thomson.** *1822-92.*
Demonstration of the variable absorption of radiant heat: **Sir John Leslie.** *1766-1832.*
Capillary action: **Sir John Leslie.** *1766-1832.*
The observation that the steam from salt water yields fresh water: **James Lind.** *1716-94.*
The chemically identical nature of carbon and diamonds: **Sir George Mackenzie.** *1780-1848.*
The electromagnetic theory of light: **James Clerk Maxwell.** *1831-79.*
The theory of feedback (cybernetics): **James Clerk Maxwell.** *1831-79.*
The kinetic theory of gases: **James Clerk Maxwell.** *1831-79.*
The observation that metals give line spectra, the basis of spectroscopy: **Thomas Melvil.** *1726-53.*
The theory of stream line flow: **William Rankine.** *1820-72.*
Open cycle refrigeration: **Lord Kelvin** and **William Rankine.** *1820-72.*
The soliton or solitary wave of translation: **John Scott Russell.** *1808-82.*
The theory of the mechanics of the prism: **Edward Sang.** *1805-90.*
Ciliary action: **William Sharpey.** *1802-80.*
Experimental proof of the existence of isotopes and their origin in radioactive processes: **Frederick Soddy.** *1877-1956.*
The chemical elucidation of the structure of the nucleic acids: **Sir Alexander Todd.** *b. 1907.*
Proposal of the proof of the earth's rotation: **Edward Sang.** *1805-90.*
The theory of evolution. Proposed independently by **Alfred Russell Wallace.** *1823-1913.*

Scottish Men of Medicine

JAMES YOUNG SIMPSON

"This is far stronger and better than ether."
James Young Simpson

Scottish Men of Medicine

So James Simpson exclaimed as he came round after his first whiff of chloroform. It is probably in the field of medicine that Scotland has had the greatest influence on the world; in clinical research; in the development of surgical techniques; in the training of generations of doctors who have then taken their expertise to all parts of the globe. The Scottish medical schools of Glasgow, Edinburgh, Aberdeen and Dundee lie behind the individual achievements of men like Lister, McEwen and Donald and of discoveries such as interferon, penicillin and chloroform. Students from all over the world came and still come to Scotland to further their medical training. Between 1751 and 1800 for example, 87% of British qualified doctors were trained in Scotland and most American doctors in the 18th century hung a certificate from Edinburgh on the walls of their consulting room. The only qualified doctor among the founders of the Harvard Medical School was an Edinburgh man.

Scottish born and trained doctors have gone on to make their mark in many diverse fields. The explorers David Livingstone and Mungo Park who opened up much of the continent of Africa to trade and Western influence were both doctors. The fate of nations has rested with people like Dr James Wylie, the only outsider present at the historic meeting of the Tsar and Napoleon at Tilsit. He was there in his capacity as the Tsar's medical attendant. Napoleon was later cared for during his exile on St Helena by another Scot, Dr Archibald Arnot. Scots doctors were frequent residents at the Russian court, Dr John Rogerson's most celebrated patient being Catherine the Great herself.

The earliest developments in Scottish medicine can be traced back to the end of the 15th century with the foundation of the first Chair in Medicine in the UK at Aberdeen. The concept of medical training rapidly spread to the other centres of learning in Scotland in the 16th century. It was Master Peter Lowe, founder of the Glasgow Faculty of Physicians and Surgeons who helped to remove surgery from the hands of the barber's trade and who also published the first textbook on surgery in the English language. The next century saw the beginnings of what were to become the great medical schools of the future, and the first application of the principles of physics and chemistry to disease. At the beginning of the century most Scottish doctors had to go abroad for training, most notably to the University of Leyden. By the end of the century, the University was inviting Scotsmen like Dr Archibald Pitcairne, to take up Chairs at Leyden. Pitcairne, a founder of the Edinburgh Medical School, completed Harvey's theory of the circulation of the blood by demonstrating that veins and arteries were linked by capillaries.

The 18th century saw Edinburgh rise to preeminence as a world centre of medical education, a reputation that it holds to this day. This was the age when the foundations of modern medical science were laid. Scots doctors played a very major part with men like Bell in neurology, Smellie in obstetrics and Pringle in military medicine. Not all of Edinburgh's reputations, however, have stood the test of time. A Lanarkshire born doctor, John Brown, developed what became

Explorer **David Livingstone** was a doctor.
ack: The David Livingstone Centre, Blantyre.

The Adam Building—the Old Royal Infirmary, Edinburgh. *1741-1879.*
ack: Lothian Health Board Archives, Edinburgh.

known as the Brunonian system. At a time, when the development of universal theories of disease was very fashionable, Brown asserted that all disease was caused by over or under stimulation of the body. For the one condition he recommended opium and for the other alcohol: personally he practised a "dose of his own medicine". His teaching caused rioting between opponents and supporters of his system in both Edinburgh and Gottingen and in Revolutionary America his theories gained many adherents, perhaps in part because of his own rise from humble origins. It was not until well into the 19th century that the Brunonian system was finally abandoned.

It has been particularly in the areas of preventive medicine, surgery and clinical techniques that Scotland has achieved preeminence.

James Lind (1716-1794)

Born and brought up in Scotland, Lind started his career as a surgeon's mate in the British navy. It was natural for him to become interested in scurvy, a disease that was endemic on long voyages. Lind studied the incidence of the disease and found that there was a common link in besieged towns, expeditionary journeys and sea voyages, in short wherever the diet was likely to be limited and monotonous. In 1747, while studying at Edinburgh University, Lind treated sailors suffering from scurvy with various diets, in what has been claimed to be the first controlled clinical experiment. He found that a diet which included lemon or lime juice was the most efficacious in the alleviation of the symptoms, followed by a diet which included drinking draughts of cider.

When Lind was appointed to be in charge of the naval hospital at Hasler in 1758, he began his lifelong crusade to convince the naval authorities to include citrus fruit as part of the staple diet. The authorities, however, were slow to react. Even when Captain Cook adopted the new treatment, and in his great expeditions of the early 1770's only lost one man in three years from scurvy, the authorities were not convinced. Even when Lind became personal physician to George III in 1783, he could not carry the point. It was only in 1795, a year after Lind's death, that the Navy, under great pressure from the war against France, adopted the practice of giving lime juice to sailors, thus earning them the nickname of "limeys".

Lind made many other contributions to the prevention of disease including the establishment of hospital ships, his advocacy of cleanliness and ventilation in sick bays and his suggestion of the supply of distilled water on ships, based on his observation that the steam from salt water yielded fresh water. These have all contributed to his title as the "Father of Naval Medicine". He also wrote the first authoritative text on tropical medicine, "The Handbook of Tropical Medicine".

It is difficult now to imagine the significance of Lind's achievements as scurvy is no longer a major scourge. His simple but effective treatment saved many thousands of lives. Fellow Scots, Sir John Pringle and Sir Gilbert Blane carried on Lind's work in putting the army and the navy on a healthy footing.

Other Scots in more recent times have played a key role in the prevention of disease. **Sir Robert Philip** developed what became known worldwide as the "Edinburgh system" for the treatment of TB based on the knowledge that it was necessary to treat the whole family of a TB victim and to tackle the environmental problems associated with the disease. He was an ardent campaigner for the introduction of mass immunisation with the BCG vaccine and for making TB a notifiable disease. It was only after years of struggle that the authorities adopted his suggestions. Another long battle with the authorities ensued before **William Boag Leishman** managed to persuade them to adopt his anti-typhoid vaccine: it was largely due to his persistence that there was no major outbreak of the disease during the First World War. In tropical medicine, **Patrick Manson** and **Ronald Ross** both Scots doctors working in the East, painstakingly traced the life cycle of the malaria parasite and paved the way for modern mosquito eradication programmes. It was Scottish medical detectives who traced the course of elephantiasis, dumdum fever and sleeping sickness.

The 18th century also saw the laying of the foundations of modern surgery, a development again largely in the hands of Scots. In the days before anaesthesia and asepsis, surgery was little more than a practical skill. With the patient fully conscious throughout an operation, great emphasis was placed on the speed at which it could be performed. Given the risks of shock and infection, amputation was often the only solution to disease or injury. Only superficial operations could be undertaken; even then, the odds against dying from infection were not good. Sir James Young Simpson showed that the death rate from infection, following amputation, in the hospital he studied was as high as five in twelve.

Alongside the Universities, private medical schools flourished and the four most eminent of these in 18th century London were all run by Scots—William Smellie's School for Obstetrics, William Cullen's School for Internal Medicine, Joseph Black's School for Chemistry and William Hunter's School for Anatomy and Surgery.

New Glasgow Royal Infirmary, Phase 1, opened 1983.
ack: Department of Medical Illustration, Glasgow Royal Infirmary.

James Lind (1716-94).
Father of Naval Medicine.
ack: The Royal College of Surgeons of Edinburgh.

Scottish Men of Medicine

John Hunter *(1728-1793).*
ack: National Galleries of Scotland, Edinburgh.

Although appreciated by contemporaries primarily for their speed with the scalpel and manual dexterity — the ultimate accolades for 18th century surgeons — William Hunter and his brother John advanced the frontiers of medical knowledge in a number of ways.

John Hunter *(1728-93)*

The son of an East Kilbride farmer, John Hunter gained the reputation as one of the greatest surgeons of the 18th century.

Although he seems to have received little formal education, as the youngest of a family of ten, he had a vast curiosity about his surroundings and spent most of his childhood exploring the local countryside. In 1748, he set off on horseback to London to join his brother William, who had already established his medical reputation. Initially, John's job was to prepare dissected anatomical specimens for use by his brother, but his skill with the scalpel was such that he was performing operations within twelve months. He spent the next eleven years studying anatomy, often using the services of the "resurrectionists" or bodysnatchers to obtain corpses. He made many original discoveries including the function of the lymph glands and the function and structure of the placenta.

In 1758 he became a teaching surgeon at St George's Hospital in London. From 1760-63 he served in the army; during this time he laid the foundations of his unique collection and also began the work that was to revolutionise surgeons' attitudes to their patients. Before Hunter, amputation was the almost universal solution to injury or disease. Hunter showed that with careful operative and post-operative treatment by the surgeon many wounds did not require this drastic remedy. In 1776 he was appointed physician extraordinary to George III.

His reputation, however, rests on more than his surgical skills. He made innovative advances in the treatment of digestive complaints, teeth, transplantation, inflammation, wounds and shock. He was the first person to suggest that blood is a living substance like other components of the body. He pioneered the art of tissue grafting, including a somewhat bizarre experiment when he grafted a human tooth on to a cock's comb. He developed what is still essentially the standard treatment for the repair of a torn tendon, operating on himself after he damaged his tendon whilst dancing. He was also a noted anatomist, making important discoveries in the fields of human and comparative anatomy and physiology.

Hunter's importance lies not only in his individual discoveries but also in his pioneering application of the principle of experimental verification. Until Hunter, little attention had been paid to pathology, the natural history of disease. A typical instance of the importance that Hunter placed on the practical verification of theory was his experiment on a deer at Richmond Park. When he tied the artery which supplied blood to one of the deer's antlers, which were in velvet, it became cold but, far from dying, within a few days the antler had regained its blood supply through the enlargement of subsidiary connecting arteries above and below the ligature. Hunter was then able to apply the treatment successfully to aneurisms in human beings.

Hunter was the physician who elevated surgery from its links with the trades of barber and butcher to its present professional status. Through his teaching, he was responsible for the establishment of surgery as an acceptable branch of medical studies in Britain, Europe and North America.

As a person, Hunter seems to have been somewhat rude and choleric in disposition. Fulfilling his own prophecy, he died from an attack of angina, to which he was subject, brought on by a fit of rage. His powers of concentration were legendary: a contemporary described him as *"standing for hours, motionless as a statue, except that with a pair of forceps in each hand he was picking asunder the connecting fibres of some object that he was studying".*

His brother, William, also made his mark on the medical world and is regarded as the founder of the modern science of gynaecology. He became the first Professor of Anatomy at the Royal Academy in 1768.

The two barriers to modern surgery were pain and infection. Both were lowered by the work of the eminent Scots practioners, Simpson and Lister.

James Young Simpson *(1811-1870)*

James Young Simpson showed his abilities early. He entered Edinburgh University at the age of 14 and his thesis, prepared as part of his medical qualification, was considered to be of such a high standard that he was immediately appointed assistant to one of the Edinburgh Professors.

In 1846, while running a large and successful medical practice in Edinburgh he became interested in the newly discovered use of ether as an anaesthetic in the United States. He experimented with ether and other anaesthetic substances among his friends. They spent many evenings round his table inhaling various potions and "noxious vapours" until he hit on chloroform which he considered to offer the best anaesthetic qualities and certainly rendered the party unconscious. He was the first person to use anaesthesia in childbirth, one Wilhelmina Carstairs being the first child to be successfully delivered by its use.

Sir James Young Simpson *(1811-1870).*
ack: The Royal College of Surgeons of Edinburgh.

Initially, the idea of anaesthesia in childbirth caused considerable controversy. Some people devoutly believed that the pain of childbirth was decreed by God as part of the curse of Eve. Simpson countered this argument by pointing out that when God created Eve from Adam's rib, he first put Adam into a "deep sleep". Simpson's views were officially vindicated when he was appointed physician to Queen Victoria and delivered her seventh child, Prince Leopold, using chloroform.

Simpson was also a noted obstetrician making major advances in the techniques of oviarotomy and in the use of obstetric forceps. He even had a prophetic streak, predicting the medical use of X-rays: *"By electrical and other lights we may render the body sufficiently diaphanous for the inspection of the practised eye of the physician or surgeon."*

It is interesting to speculate that but for Simpson, another Scot might have achieved more prominence in the alleviation of pain. It was **James Esdale** from Perth who in a hospital in India, achieved the first successful operation using the technique of hypnosis. The development was not, however, followed up because of the success of ether and chloroform. Even the word "hypnosis" was coined by a Scot!

One of the greatest surgeons in terms of skill, innovation and teaching was James Syme, whose career spanned the introduction of anaesthesia. Indeed some of his patients must have had cause to regret his rather choleric temperament as due to a disagreement with Simpson, he was slow to adopt the new techniques.

James Syme (1799-1870)

Syme was born within sight of the castle in Edinburgh, the city which was to be his home for virtually all of his life. Perhaps it was its influence that later earned him the title of "the Napoleon of Medicine".

A childhood friend was Robert Christison, who later, as Professor of Materia Medica at Edinburgh University was to write the first work on toxicology in the English language. Together they formed with some fellow students a club which met weekly to carry out chemical experiments. It was there at the age of 18 that Syme discovered the effective solvent for india rubber that was later to be used with such commercial effect by Macintosh.

In 1818 while studying medicine at Edinburgh University Syme became assistant and demonstrator to the great anatomist Robert Liston, whose splint is still used today. When Liston resigned in 1823, Syme took over the teaching of his classes. He quickly established himself as a surgeon, specialising in the amputation of tubercular joints, the technique of which he pioneered. One of his most dramatic operations involved the removal of a sarcoma from a diseased jaw. In the days before anaesthesia, this twenty-four minute operation must have been excruciating for the patient but he reported fit for work again within five weeks.

At first Syme, according to the normal practice, performed operations largely in the homes of his patients. The demand for his skills, however, was so great, coupled with his growing concern about the risks of operations in unhygienic surroundings—the kitchen table doubled up as the operating table—that in 1829 he opened his own surgical hospital in Edinburgh.

Although the most successful surgeon of his day, Syme also found time for research and writing. In 1831 he published his "Treatise on the Excision of Diseased Joints" which set out to raise the techniques of amputation from the level of the butcher's shop to that of science. In the same year, he published his "Principles of Surgery". In 1833 after a sharp contest with his old supervisor Liston, Syme was appointed to the Chair of Clinical Surgery at the University where he immediately set out to reform the existing methods of clinical teaching. He introduced the modern practice of having students present at consultations with patients in order to develop their diagnostic skills.

Syme continued to extend his surgical techniques developing an effective operation for aneurism and the operation for amputation of the ankle joint which still bears his name. His clinical researches included the demonstration of the ability of periosteum to form new bone. His work as a surgeon bridged the period of the introduction of anaesthesia which he eventually adopted for his operations although this was delayed owing to a quarrel with James Young Simpson. Syme's quarrel with Simpson was a typical incident as Syme was graced with a somewhat disputatious temperament. When Simpson, in Syme's eyes only an obstetrician, ventured to suggest that Syme should adopt acupressure as a means of controlling surgical haemorrhage, Syme did not simply reject his advice. While operating before an assembled class of students, he called for an operating knife, cut Simpson's pamphlet on the subject into shreds, ground them into the sawdust with his foot and commented *"there, gentlemen, is what acupressure is worth".*

In the days before antiseptic surgery, Syme, conscious of the risks of infection, developed one of the most successful preventive techniques, that of leaving wounds completely open until the oozing of blood had ceased. It was his successor in the Edinburgh Chair, his son-in-law Joseph Lister, who was to tackle the root of the problem.

James Syme (1799-1870).
ack: The Royal College of Surgeons of Edinburgh.

Joseph Lister (1827-1912)

Although by birth an Englishman it was while working in Glasgow that Lister pioneered the concept of antiseptic surgery. His early interests were in amputation and the new technique of anaesthesia. These developments, however, were of no avail in many cases as the patient died soon after of infection. His concern was heightened by the knowledge that his ward at Glasgow's Royal Infirmary was built on top of the common graveyard used for the burial of cholera victims.

In 1865, learning of Pasteur's research into the micro-organisms that cause disease, it occurred to Lister to try to kill germs in wounds by treatment with chemicals. He used carbolic acid and the death rate dropped dramatically. He covered everything in the operating theatre with carbolic acid—wounds, dressings and instruments. He devised a spray which sent a fine mist of carbolic acid into the air above the patient. By these means he was able to undertake more ambitious operations involving deeper incisions than had previously been possible.

Lister did not stop in the operating theatre in his quest for the eradication of infection. He was the first person to use dressings sterilised by heat and to experiment with the use of tincture of iodine to sterilise the skin; he also introduced absorbent gauze dressings. Of great significance was his discovery of the sterile catgut ligature which became absorbed by the tissues of the patient and so did not form a source of irritation and sepsis like the silk ligatures in use at the time. He experimented by tying the carotid artery of a calf which was killed a month later: on dissection it was discovered that the catgut was gone and replaced by a circle of living fibrous tissue. Despite a personal appeal from Queen Victoria, Lister went on to testify to the Royal Commission on Vivisection that his results could not have been achieved without animal experimentation.

Lister was a prophet crying in the wilderness as far as his native country was concerned. German surgeons were quick to adopt his new ideas but in both Britain and America surgeons were unconvinced. They had tried his methods without success, they claimed. One of America's greatest surgeons, J M T Finney, writing of the Massachusetts General Hospital in 1888, revealed the reason why. Despite Lister's stress that all items in the operating theatre must be kept free of infection, surgeons still operated in frock coats, often stiff with blood and age, the status symbol of the surgical profession. The instruments had wooden handles which were at best given a perfunctory wipe with carbolic solution and the sponges used to swab operative wounds were used over and over again. It took a new generation of American surgeons to adopt the Listerian message in its entirety and their example at last convinced the British medical profession.

Lister was created a peer in 1883 and became the first medical man to be elevated to the House of Lords. He also succeeded Lord Kelvin as President of the Royal Society.

Joseph Lister (1827-1912).
ack: The Royal College of Surgeons of Edinburgh.

Lister's Carbolic Spray.   ack: People's Palace Museum, Glasgow.

Simpson and Lister bequeathed to the surgeons who came after them two vital legacies, the ability to work at a less frenetic pace and to investigate deep into the body's tissue without the risk of subsequent death from infection. One of the greatest pioneers of the "new" surgery was Sir William McEwen.

Sir William McEwen (1848-1924)

The son of a Rothesay merchant, William McEwen rose to become Professor of Surgery at his alma mater of Glasgow University and one of the founders of modern surgical practice.

In many ways McEwen capitalised on Lister's advances which had made possible long and complex surgery. He evolved many of the techniques of brain surgery, introduced the operation for mastoid, conducted the first bone graft operation and devised an effective operation for the correction of knock knees. He performed the first operation for the excision of a lung: until McEwen's time it was believed that the opening of the chest would result in the collapse of the lungs.

In 1880 McEwen demonstrated that periosteum was not the only source of new bone. He had as a patient a boy whose upper arm had been almost entirely destroyed by the disease osteomyelitis. Acting on his knowledge gained through experimentation with animals, McEwen removed a series of bony wedges from the boy's shin bone and embedded them in a row in the muscles of his arm. The bones knitted together to give the boy once more a useful and functioning arm. Thus began the techniques of bone graft surgery.

McEwen was a man of vision. He realised, for example, the importance of nursing in post surgical cases and with the Matron of the Royal Infirmary of Glasgow devised the first systematic training course for nursing staff. His concept of patient care was total.

The innovative tradition of Scots surgery has been carried on into the 20th century with the work of men like Ian Aird, who headed the research team that pioneered the heart lung machine and kidney transplants in the UK. His interests and talents were wide-ranging; he performed the first successful operation to separate Siamese twins in the UK and undertook pioneering research in the relationship between disease and blood groupings, the implications of which are still being followed through today.

In the development of drugs to treat disease, Scots have also played a key role both at home and overseas. John MacLeod who was awarded the Nobel Prize for his work on the isolating of insulin and its use in the treatment of diabetes was of Scots descent as was William Morton, the first person to operate using anaesthesia. It was due to more than coincidence that Edinburgh became a world ranking centre for the manufacture of morphine and chloroform, as it was William Gregory who first prepared pure forms of both. The drug that has

Sir William McEwen (1848-1924).
ack: The Royal College of Surgeons of Edinburgh.

revolutionised 20th century medicine—penicillin—was first discovered by a Scot.

Sir Alexander Fleming (1881-1955)

Born in Dalry in Ayrshire, Alexander Fleming was educated at Kilmarnock High School. After working for five years in London as a shipping clerk, he won a scholarship to study medicine at the University of London where he proved to be a brilliant student. From the beginning his main interest lay in bacteriology and he pioneered the introduction to Britain of salvarsan, an efficient killer of spirochetes, the micro-organism that causes syphilis.

While serving in the Royal Army Medical Corps during the First World War Fleming began the research which was to lead to his discovery in 1922 of the protein, lysozyme—a protein found, for example, in tears, which has bacteria killing properties.

It was while Fleming, by now Professor of Bacteriology at St Mary's Medical School where he had trained as a student, was working in his research laboratory that he "accidentally" discovered penicillin. He returned from a month's holiday in 1928 to discover that one of the culture plates that he had left in a dark corner in the laboratory displayed unusual characteristics. There was an absence of staphylococcal colonies in the vicinity of the mould that had grown on the plate. After an intensive investigation, Fleming read a paper giving the first news of his discovery to a meeting of the Medical Research Club in 1929. Audience reaction was nil.

The first clinical application of crude penicillin was made by Fleming in 1929 when he treated his assistant, Stuart Craddock, for an infected antrum by washing out the sinus with a diluted penicillin broth. The treatment was largely effective.

Fleming, however, was no chemist and could not isolate or identify the substance that he had named penicillin. It was only the impetus of the Second World War, with the realisation that the discovery of new anti-bacterials would be crucial to the treatment of wounded soldiers, that set Florey and Chain to work to isolate the substance. They succeeded and it proved to be as successful as Fleming's first experiments suggested. In 1944, Fleming was awarded a Knighthood for his

Sir Alexander Fleming *(1881-1955).*
At his bench in St Mary's Hospital Paddington, London *(1908).*
ack: Audio Visual Department, St Mary's Medical School, Paddington, London.

work and in 1945 he shared with Florey and Chain the Nobel Prize for medicine.

The Scottish tradition of innovation in drug development continues with the work of people like Dr Black on Beta blockers. It was also a Scot who may or may not have provided medicine with a future revolution.

Alick Isaacs (1921-1967)

Isaacs may in future centuries win a place as one of the greatest alleviators of human disease or his discovery may be overtaken by other developments. Only time will tell. This does not detract from the quality of his research or the depth of his innovative mind.

Alick Isaacs, the discoverer of interferon, was born in Glasgow where he graduated in medicine from the University after a brilliant student career during which he won all the major medical prizes. His early years as a researcher in the Department of Bacteriology of the University, although involved with very different areas of research than that of his subsequent work, convinced him that research rather than medical practice or teaching was his chosen destiny.

It was during a year spent with Professor C H Stuart Harris at Sheffield University that Isaac's interest in virology was first aroused. He won a Rockefeller scholarship to continue his research at the University of Melbourne where Sir Macfarlane Burnet's group was undertaking exciting work on the influenza virus. On his return to the UK, he was put in charge of the World Influenza Centre laboratory at the National Institute for Medical Research. There he studied antigenic variations in influenza viruses while continuing his

Alick Isaacs (1921-1967).
ack: Times Newspapers Limited.

Interferon (phials of interferon used in the treatment of cancer).
ack: Royal Hospital for Sick Children and Queen Mother's Hospital, Glasgow.

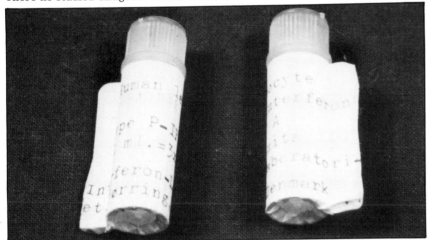

research on viral interference which was to lead to his discovery of interferon.

After years of painstaking research, with the collaboration of a Swiss visiting researcher, Dr J Lindemann, Isaacs published in 1957 the original description of interferon. He showed the phenomenon of viral interference to be the result of the action of a cellular factor induced in the course of virus infection and capable of inhibiting virus multiplication. His discovery led to a renewed medical interest in viral interference and resulted in doctors and scientists now having a much greater degree of understanding of the complex process of viral multiplication.

Isaacs was not only a dedicated and brilliant researcher: he was a man of immense kindness and fun. He derived as much pleasure from the introduction of interferon into the Flash Gordon cartoon strip as from many scientific tributes and honours. Tragically, he died at the early age of 45 while the full implications of his work were still being assessed. Whether interferon turns out to be the wonder drug of the 20th century with potential for attacking diseases from cancer to the common cold is still in the future. Whatever the outcome, Isaacs will have made a major contribution to the development of virology.

Scotland's long industrial tradition has also played its part in the development of medical innovation. Glasgow's cotton industry, for example, indirectly gave rise to the use of cotton wool in the treatment of wounds.

Dr Alexander Anderson (1794-1871)

This Glasgow doctor had as a patient the daughter of a local textile worker. He was called to the house one day because the child had fallen into a pot of boiling porridge; in her panic, the mother who worked from home as a cotton spinner had wrapped her child in the first thing that came to hand, a wad of processed cotton awaiting spinning.

From earliest times, raw cotton had been used as a means of staunching wounds. Its use, however, had been discredited by the medical profession on the grounds that it contained bugs and bacteria that caused more harm than the treatment did good. From the 17th century onwards, rags were standardly used in Europe to bind wounds. Anderson observed, however, that his patient's scalds had already begun to heal and he then conducted a series of trials using processed cotton wool, culminating in an article in the Glasgow Medical Journal of 1828

Alexander Anderson (1794-1871).
ack: The Royal College of Physicians and Surgeons of Glasgow.

recommending the adoption of its use in the treatment of burns. Not a major breakthrough perhaps but rather an instance of the application of observation and sound common sense.

A breakthrough of a much more radical nature, linking in with Scotland's engineering heritage, is pregnancy scanning.

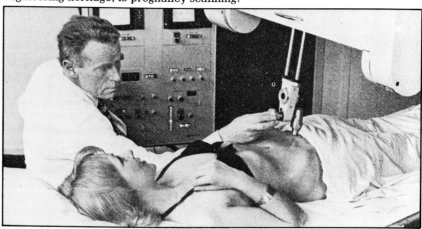

Ian Donald 1910-.
Using the pregnancy scanner.
ack: Ian Donald and Messrs Lloyd-Luke (Medical Books) Limited.

Ian Donald *(1910-)*

It was in 1954 that Donald arrived in Glasgow to take up a teaching appointment with only, what he modestly refers to as, an elementary knowledge of radar from his days in the Royal Airforce, and a *"continuing childish interest in machines, electronic or otherwise, or what my wife would refer to as my toys"*.

He developed an interest in the emergent study of ultrasonics as a diagnostic technique. Several doctors in the United States had pioneered the technique but the only way that they could get results was by immersing the patient in a tank of water. This had obvious drawbacks. Donald realised the answer might lie in the techniques used in the detection of flaws in metals where probes coated with oil were applied directly to the material under test. He was introduced to scientists on the staff of the Clydeside plant of Babcock and Wilcox who were building boilers for nuclear power stations. Using their ultrasonic metal detecting devices, he experimented to see if he could trace any difference in various forms of pelvic tumour. In 1955 he took a memorable trip to the factory with various specimens to test and a lump of steak to use as a control. The screens showed up the differences and opened up endless possibilities to Donald's fertile mind.

He immediately set to work to make these a reality. At first the equipment was clumsy and improvised, the improvisations including the use of a contraceptive sheath. This inadvertently gave the project some unexpected publicity through the circulation of the following story. A medical friend of Donald's who was on a visit from South Africa volunteered to purchase some supplies on the grounds that he was not known in Glasgow; he was so non-plussed when the shop assistant asked him what type he wanted, he replied that he would need to go over to the car to find out! Once the technical problems were overcome, Donald's next task was to overcome the scepticism of his colleagues. This he finally did with the saving of a patient whose case had previously been diagnosed as terminal, through use of the scanner to correct a misdiagnosis.

In 1957 Donald turned his attention to the use of the scanner in pregnancy. With the help of a Glasgow engineering firm, he developed a two-dimensional scanner and in 1958 went public with his results. Further developments such as the use of Polaroid photography to provide detailed results at the patient's bedside followed rapidly, culminating in the unveiling of an automatic scanner in 1960. Donald's work allowed the course of pregnancy to be studied from beginning to end with the resultant increase in the health of both mother and the baby-to-be. Indeed one of Donald's associates identified a case of quintuplets at nine weeks in 1970. Nowadays pregnancy scanning is a standard screening process for the expectant mother, allowing doctors to monitor the growth of the unborn child and to identify any abnormalities or potential difficulties with the actual birth well in advance.

Scotland has maintained its pioneering role in scanning techniques with a number of companies active in the design and development of scanners. After twelve years of research at Aberdeen University, **Professor Mallard** set up his own company to develop his pioneering research into NMR techniques. His scanner is currently undergoing clinical trials in an Edinburgh hospital.

Scots continue to make their mark on many branches of medicine. The continuing work on leukaemia by the Glasgow research team where the feline leukaemia virus was first isolated....the world's first laboratory-developed human monoclonal antibody of enormous potential in the treatment of virus related disease....slow acting drugs that release doses internally over a period of time....new materials based on seaweed for use in post operative healing.... only the future will tell.

Increasing man's knowledge of his body

Discovery of the distinct functions of the brain: **Sir Charles Bell.** *1774-1842.*
Description of the fold of the peritoneum: **James Douglas.** *1675-1742.*
Elucidation of the disease, Bell's palsy: **Sir Charles Bell.** *1774-1842.*
The medicinal value of cod liver oil: **John Hughes Bennett.** *1812-75.*
Identification of the cause of brucellosis and sleeping sickness: **Sir David Bruce.**
Efficacy of amyl nitrate in treatment of angina: **Sir Thomas Brunton.**
1844-1916.
The process of respiration: **John Cheyne.** *1777-1836.*
Isolation of the active principle of hemlock: **Robert Christison.** *1797-1882.*
Description of pernicious anaemia: **James Combe.** *1796-1883.*
Relationship of parts of the brain to the movement of particular limbs: **Sir David Ferrier.** *1843-1928.*
Description of the blood disease, leucocythaemia: **John Hughes Bennett.** *1812-75.*
Investigation of snake venoms and their antidotes: **Sir Thomas Fraser.** *1841-1920.*
The demonstration of the transmission of puerperal fever: **D N Gordon.** *1795.*
Development of the stage decompression technique still used in the treatment of divers with bends: **John Haldane.** *1860-1936.*
The theory of the association of ideas and unconscious mental modification: **Sir William Hamilton.** *1788-1856.*
Identification of the parasite involved in dum-dum fever: **Sir William Boag Leishman.** *1865-1926.*
The use of lemon juice as a specific against scurvy: **James Lind.** *1716-94.*
Hypnotism for the treatment of shellshock: **Dr McDougall.**
The systematic treatment of heart disease: **Sir James MacKenzie.** *1853-1925.*
The lifecycle of the malaria parasite: **Sir Patrick Manson.** *1844-1922:* and **Sir Ronald Ross.** *1857-1932.*
The description of the prolapsed intervertebral cartilage (slipped disc): **George Middleton.** *1853-1923.*
The distinction between the diseases, typhus and typhoid: **Robert Perry.** *1783-1848.*
Identification of the clinical symptoms of hypothermia: **James Lind.** *1716-94.*
The naming and identification of the staphylococcus bacteria: **Sir Alexander Oghton.** *1844-1929.*
Tracing of the lifecycle of the elephantiasis parasite: **Sir Patrick Manson.** *1844-1922.*
The foramen of Monro: **Alexander Monro.** *1733-1817.*
Demonstration that the veins and arteries are linked by capillaries: **Archibald Pitcairne.** *1652-1713.*
The significance of the putrefactive process in spreading disease: **Sir John Pringle.** *1707-82.*
The Argyll Robertson pupil reaction: **Douglas Argyll Robertson.** *1837-1909.*
Recognition of the substance which controls sugar metabolism: **Edward Sharpey-Schaffer.** *1850-1935.*
Use of nitrous acid to prevent the spread of contagion: **James Smyth.** *1741-1821.*
The vaccine against the herpes virus: **Gordon Skinner.**
Demonstration of the power of periosteum to form new bone: **James Syme.** *1799-1870.*
First clinical descriptions of diphtheria and tuberculous meningitis: **Robert Whytt.** *1714-66.*
The importance of leaving wounds open until they have ceased to bleed: **James Syme.** *1799-1870.*
Identification of the seat of reflex action: **Robert Whytt.** *1714-66.*

Medical institutions

The first clinic for mental outpatient treatment: **Robert Dick Gillespie.** *1897-1945.*
The first hospital X-ray unit: Glasgow. *1896.*
The founder of the first School of Neurology: **Sir James Crighton Browne.** *1840-1938.*
The first training scheme for psychiatric nursing: Dumfries. *1854.*
The first TB clinic: Edinburgh. **Sir Robert Philip.** *1854-1939.*
The first public lunatic asylum for the humane treatment of the mentally ill: **Andrew Duncan.** *1807.*
Ante-natal clinics: **John Ballantyne.** *1861-1923.*
The hospital ship: **Sir Gilbert Blane.** *1749-1834.*
The world's first radiological department: **John MacIntyre.** *1857-1928.*

Medical technology

The first doctor to advocate the use of cotton wool: *1828.* **Dr. Alexander Anderson.** *1794-1871.*

The first iron lung in the UK: Designed by **Robert Henderson** in Aberdeen. *1933.*

Foetal screening tests for spina bifida and cystic fibrosis: **David Brock.**

Popularisation of the use of the clinical thermometer: **James Currie.** *1756-1801.*

Pregnancy scanning: **Ian Donald.** *1910-.*

The application of HOT techniques to victims of carbon monoxide poisoning: **Dr. George Smith.**

The application of HOT techniques for the treatment of "blue babies": **Dr. James Hutchinson.** *1912-.*

The first practicable ultrasonic scanner: **Ian Donald.** *1910-.*

Absorbent gauze dressings: **Joseph Lister.** *1827-1912.*

X-ray techniques applied to the heart, lungs, spine and the inside of the skull: **John MacIntyre.** *1857-1928.*

Axis-traction midwifery forceps: **Alexander Simpson.** *1835-1916.*

Chloroform as an anaesthetic: **Sir James Young Simpson.** *1808-59.*

Probe pointed surgical scissors: **Joseph Lister.** *1827-1912.*

Bone cutting forceps: **Robert Liston.** *1794-1847.*

The polygraph: **Sir James MacKenzie.** *1853-1925.*

The introduction of the hypodermic syringe into general practice: **Alexander Wood.** *1817-84.*

The Liston splint: **Robert Liston.** *1794-1847.*

The sinus forceps: **Joseph Lister.** *1827-1912.*

Catgut ligature for surgery: **Joseph Lister.** *1827-1912,*

Operations by Scots surgeons

The Caesarian section in cases where the pelvis is distorted: **Murdoch Cameron.** *1880's.*

The first successful operation using hypnosis: **James Esdale.** *1845.*

The first public operation on a patient under general anaesthesia: **Robert Liston.** *1846.*

The first amputation using anaesthesia: **William Scott.** *1846.*

The first separation of Siamese twins in the UK: **Ian Aird.** *1905-62.*

The modern techniques of Caesarian section: **John Kerr.**

The development of kidney transplants: **Ian Aird.** *1905-62.*

The removal of the scapula (shoulder blade): **Robert Liston.** *1794-1847.*

Several techniques in brain surgery: **Sir William McEwen.** *1848-1924.*

The excision of tubercular joints: **James Syme.** *1799-1870.*

The standard operation for mastoid: **Sir William McEwen.** *1848-1924.*

The first bone graft operation: **Sir William McEwen.** *1848-1924.*

The first operations involving plastic surgery: **James Syme.** *1799-1870.*

The operation for the correction of knock knees: **Sir William McEwen.** *1848-1924.*

The Engineering Giants

LORD KELVIN

"The life and soul of science is its practical application."
William Thomson, Lord Kelvin

The Engineering Giants

Sir William Fairbairn *(1789-1874)*
ack: The Mansell Collection, London.

Lord Kelvin certainly practised what he preached. Not only did he undertake fundamental work in physics but he also applied it to his work on telegraphy, to the instruments that he designed, to his ideas for heat pumps and for harnessing the power of the Niagara Falls. Truly, he was a practical man of science.

This tempering of scientific theory with the practical realism of the Scot in part accounts for the remarkable number and quality of Scottish engineers. The small size of Scotland has lent itself, as with her scientists, to a continuous interaction between the Universities and the practitioners—an interaction which has borne remarkable fruit in men such as James Watt and Lord Kelvin.

Yet if one looks at the background of Scotland's engineers, they are remarkably varied. Sir William Fairbairn, one of the first structural engineers, was the son of a farm servant whereas James Nasmyth's formative years were shaped by the artistic circles of the capital city. As with most branches of Scottish innovation, the parish manse provided the background to, and more surprisingly in a few cases, the calling of several major engineers. As the engineering industry evolved from the skills of the millwright and the blacksmith, so did many of the new professionals come from those same craft backgrounds.

In the centuries before the great impetus of the Industrial Revolution, most engineers were purely practical men. They devised practical solutions to practical problems. It was James Smith of Deanston's interest in draining his land that inspired him to invent the subsoil plough. The two Scots, Michael Menzies and Andrew Meikle, who invented and developed the threshing machine were respectively the local blacksmith and the local millwright.

It was ironically not a Scot, but an Englishman who spent most of his working life in Scotland, John Roebuck, who first rose to the challenge of shaping Scotland's natural resources towards its engineering future. Iron in Scotland was at the time only smelted in negligible quantities and using methods which had not changed much since the Iron Age. He established the Carron Iron Works in 1760 and turned his ingenuity and the fruits of his contacts with chemists like William Cullen and Joseph Black, to devising a more efficient fuel for smelting than the traditional charcoal. He was soon able to utilise the much cheaper and efficient local coal and the foundry grew from strength to strength. In 1779, it started to manufacture, and incidentally gave the name to, a naval gun, the carronade, which was the staple of the British Navy for the next century.

It was undoubtedly Scotland's natural resources that helped her to win such a leading role in the Industrial Revolution. The raw materials of the engineering industry—ample seams of iron and coal, access to water to drive machinery, and to seas to export the final products around the world—were all plentiful. It took ingenuity, however, to turn these resources into suitable forms for the engineering workshops; to mine the coal, to smelt the iron, to power the furnaces. The Scots responded to the call for ingenuity.

Iron and Steel: The Raw Materials of Engineering.

The first to respond was **David Mushet** *(1772-1847)*, who as manager of the Coatbridge Iron Works, discovered in 1800 a way of making effective use of the local black band ironstone in smelting. The twin advantages of a local source of supply and the deep waters of the Clyde made a major contribution to the West of Scotland's growing reputation as a workshop to the world. Mushet also discovered, about the same time, a direct process for making steel from bar iron. One of the greatest metallurgists of his day, he played a major role in the development of a systematic approach to the technologies of metal manufacture.

It was an employee of the Wilsontown Iron Works, **James Condie,** who in the 1830's devised the water cooled tuyère, known as the Scottish tuyère, which allowed for the expansion of the size of blast furnaces. It soon became a standard piece of equipment in the industry.

James Neilson *(1792-1865)*, the son of a Glasgow millwright, worked as superintendent of a Glasgow gas works. He made an innovative contribution to his chosen calling by devising a means of removing the sulphur from gas and by inventing the fishtail gas burner, the standard gas fitment of the early Victorian household. Poor as the light from his burner was, by modern standards, it was a vast improvement on the crude whale oil lamps, candles and rushlights of earlier generations and in its small way contributed to the marked increase in literacy of the period.

It is, however, with his discovery of the hot blast, that Neilson made his most lasting contribution to the economy and indeed health of the 19th century. Previously the flourishing iron industry paid little heed to either the surrounding environment or to fuel efficiency. The flames and smoke that surrounded the furnaces, the sight of which caused fellow Scot, James Nasmyth to despair that

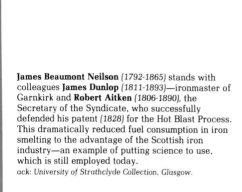

James Beaumont Neilson *(1792-1865)* stands with colleagues **James Dunlop** *(1811-1893)*—ironmaster of Garnkirk and **Robert Aitken** *(1806-1890)*, the Secretary of the Syndicate, who successfully defended his patent *(1828)* for the Hot Blast Process. This dramatically reduced fuel consumption in iron smelting to the advantage of the Scottish iron industry—an example of putting science to use, which is still employed today.
ack: University of Strathclyde Collection, Glasgow.

"Vulcan had driven out Ceres" were due to several erroneous beliefs held by the ironmasters. Although they were aware that ninety per cent of the coke that they used to fuel the furnaces was wasted, they believed that leaving the mouth of the furnace open gave the iron an improved quality as did blasting it with cold air.

Neilson demonstrated the advantages both in terms of efficiency and fuel economy of using heated air in the furnace: his methods resulted in a tripling of the quantity of iron that could be produced for a given amount of fuel. By 1860 ninety per cent of Britain's iron output used the hot blast technique. It was not, however, without great personal cost that Neilson won the day. His patents were challenged by a local ironmaster who had been quick to see the advantages of Neilson's method but did not want to pay for them. It was only after a bitter and expensive struggle that Neilson emerged victorious with his patents secured.

Robert Mushet *(1811-1891)* was not so lucky. His neglect of his patent rights allowed others to benefit from his discovery of cast steel. The Bessemer process of steel manufacture had originally been hailed as a major breakthrough but the inability to produce quality metal using the process quickly led to its becoming increasingly discredited. It was denounced by The Times as *"a brilliant meteor that had flashed across the metallurgical horizon"*. It was Bessemer's lack of metallurgical knowledge that led him to announce his discovery when the battle was only half won. It was Robert Mushet's metallurgical bent, handed down from his father, that led him to perfect the process.

The owner of a small iron foundry in Gloucestershire, he realised that the faults in the steel produced by the Bessemer process were due largely to excess oxygen in the metal which made it crack when exposed to strong heat. His solution was simple, the addition of manganese ore to the melt which attracted away the excess oxygen. Indeed so simple was this solution that few were prepared to believe Mushet and he had to install a Bessemer plant in his foundry and produce ingots of cast steel before the sceptics accepted his theory. As a further demonstration of the strength of cast steel, he forged the first all-steel railway track which was laid at Derby station. Ten years later in 1867, he requested of the railway company that the rail should be taken out to inspect how well it had worn. The company refused on the grounds that an average of 500 trains a day passed over it! Sadly, although Bessemer became a millionaire, the same fate did not await the man who had come to his rescue at a critical time. Bessemer paid Mushet a small annuity for his trouble but took all the credit himself.

Not only were raw materials necessary to support the rapid industrial growth of Britain in the late 18th century, efficient means of transporting men and goods had also to be there. The profession of architect had already been established. The new industrialists could call on William Adam and his like to build them an elegant country house. Before, however, they achieved the level of prosperity to afford such gentlemanly affectations, they needed roads that were more than cart tracks, bridges that crossed rivers at the nearest point, ports to provide safe anchor for their ships. Two men appeared to impose the disciplines of science on the craft of building and thereby to create a new profession, civil engineering. They were **John Rennie** *(1761-1821)* whose achievements include Waterloo Bridge in London, Glasgow docks and the Kennet and Avon canal, and Thomas Telford, who spanned the age from horse to steam.

John Rennie *(1761-1821).*
ack: National Galleries of Scotland, Edinburgh.

The Engineering Giants

Thomas Telford (1757-1834).
ack: National Portrait Gallery, London.

Thomas Telford (1757-1834)

Born and brought up in Eskdale in Dumfriesshire, Telford rose from humble beginnings to become one of the first great civil engineers.

In his capacity as Surveyor of Public Works in the county of Shropshire, Telford developed the system of turnpike roads. His improvements, combined with his rising reputation, led him to be appointed in 1803 to direct the development and construction of roads in the Highlands of Scotland in an effort to advance the economy of the region and to bring it closer to the main centres of population. During the next eighteen years Telford supervised the building of 920 miles of new roads in Scotland and of 1117 bridges. He used 120 contractors for the building programme under contracts with rigid specifications. In doing so, he brought the contract system to approximately that which is used today.

Telford's most notable work as a road engineer, however, was the improvement of the Holyhead road which was the main link with Ireland and ran through North Wales. His crowning achievement was the bridge across the Menai Straits. His route from London to Holyhead has no slope more than one in twenty and for alignment and gradient cannot be surpassed today. Telford has justifiably been described as the Rolls Royce of road engineers.

Telford lived through the heyday of the canal boom and his contributions to canal building include the first aqueduct to use cast iron, the great Pontcysyllte aqueduct carrying the Shropshire Union Canal on nineteen cast iron arches supported by masonry piers 121 feet high, and the Caledonian Canal between Inverness and Fort William, designed to save shipping the long and perilous journey round the north coast of Scotland. Telford's building of the Gotha Canal in Sweden to provide a link between the North Sea and the Baltic was an early example of the export of British engineering skill to which the Scots were to make such a major contribution.

Telford was involved as engineer or consultant in a multiplicity of other building projects including St Katherine's Dock in London where steam pumps driven by two engines of 80hp each were used to maintain the water level of the dock. Telford ordered the pumps from *"my friend, Mr James Watt and his able and ingenious assistant Mr Murdoch"*. He lived long enough to see the dawn of the railway age, being called in both by Parliament and by some of the earliest railway companies to advise on the proposed routes.

In addition to his work as engineer, Telford also made a major contribution to the establishment of a civil engineering profession. He was a firm believer in early surveying and planning of projects, and in contractual agreements written in clear, unambiguous English. His approach raised the standards operated by building contractors and also attracted to him a generation of younger engineers who were able and ambitious. Many "Telford trained" engineers went on to become the master engineers of the coming railway age.

Telford's design for St Katherine's Dock might not have proved possible without the assistance of the steam pumps designed by Mr Watt. One can go much further. Many of the achievements of the 19th century whether in industry, transport or the acquisition of an Empire might not have been possible if one man had not sat down to repair a model and risen again with the power to drive it.

Thomas Telford—Caledonian Canal, series of nine locks, Neptune's Staircase (near Fort William).
ack: Anthony MacMillan, Fort William.

James Watt *(1736-1819)*

James Watt was brought up in Greenock, the Clyde port and shipbuilding centre. His childhood was tinged with sadness. His mother died when he was in his teens and his father, once a prosperous merchant, experienced a downturn in his business affairs. Like many young Scots before and since, he went south to seek his fortune. He was apprenticed to an instrument maker in London for a year. In 1756 he returned to Scotland and tried to establish himself as an instrument maker but he fell foul of the municipal authorities as lacking a sufficiently long apprenticeship. He succeeded eventually in gaining employment at Glasgow University, which was outwith the municipal jurisdiction.

A number of factors were at work to result in his perfection of the steam engine. He came into contact with Joseph Black and learned of his work on latent heat. He had a unique opportunity to study the workings of the Newcomen engine when the University gave him a model to mend after a London instrument maker had failed, and to realise its inefficiency and limitations.

It was during a Sunday walk on Glasgow Green that the idea came to him as to how to improve the Newcomen engine. His solution was the introduction of a condenser, a chamber into which the steam could be led and which could be kept cool while the first chamber or cylinder was kept permanently hot. In this way the two processes were not forced to cancel each other out. In 1769, he patented his steam engine.

Over the next few years Watt made many improvements to his design and in 1774 went into partnership with Matthew Boulton, a wealthy Birmingham businessman, to manufacture steam engines for sale. By 1790 the Watt engine had replaced the Newcomen engine entirely and by 1800 some five hundred were at work in England. In fact so effective was the Watt engine that many give him sole credit for the invention of the steam engine arguing that the Newcomen engine was essentially only a pump.

In the 1780's Watt's fertile mind continued to power the steam revolution. He invented "steam heat" in 1784, using steam pipes to heat his office. He devised mechanical attachments to his engine that converted the up and down movement of a piston into the rotary motion of a wheel. This versatility allowed iron founders to operate bellows and textile manufacturers to drive looms. Just when industrialists were beginning to look at the mechanisation of industrial processes, Watt's invention was right for the times.

The consequences of Watt's invention were incalculable. He provided the prime mover for the Industrial Revolution. Factories no longer needed to be tied to locations where there was a strong source of water power. Massive machines could be built and housed in factories, ushering in the Victorian era of mass production.

Watt also produced the first germ of automation with his invention of the centrifugal governor which automatically controlled the engine's output of steam. Indeed it is the Greek word for governor, that provided the name for the later science of cybernetics, named and developed by another Scot, James Clerk Maxwell.

Watt also has a place in the history of measurement. By taking a strong horse he found that it could raise a 150lb weight nearly four feet in one second, thus providing the definition of "horsepower". The equivalent unit of power in the metric system is named the watt in honour of him.

James Watt steam engine.
Early model steam engine featuring Watt's separate condenser. Model used by Watt.
ack: Museum of Transport, Glasgow.

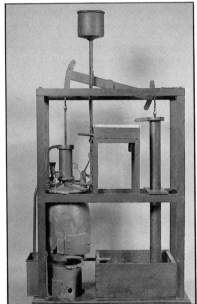

James Watt the Newcomen engine.
ack: The Hunterian Museum, University of Glasgow.

Statue of James Watt, Matthew Boulton and William Matthew Boulton by William Bloye.
ack: The Birmingham Post.

Watt has many other claims to fame. He invented the revolution counter, was one of the first people to use a slide rule, developed the principle of the gasometer, proposed the screw propeller over sixty years before it came into use and was even the first person to reverse a marine engine. Sir Humphrey Davy was moved to liken him to Archimedes.

There were in fact three men, not one, who provided the motive power for Britain's engineering potential. Watt and his steam engine, Neilson and the hot blast, and an artist's son who turned his creative imagination to the steam hammer rather than the paint brush.

James Nasmyth (1808-1890)

The son of the Scottish portrait painter and architect Alexander Nasmyth, Nasmyth inherited his father's talents but put them to a different use. He became interested in engineering while still in his teens in Edinburgh and by the age of seventeen, was capable of building model steam engines.

Like many before and since, Nasmyth was attracted by the magnetic pull of London and he served his apprenticeship in the workshop of Henry Maudslay, himself a pioneer of many early developments in machine tools. In 1834, he returned to Edinburgh winning several local commissions as an engineer. Three years later, however, he decided to move to Manchester which at the time was a burgeoning industrial centre. On the outskirts of the city he built what later became known as the Bridgewater Foundry, for the manufacture of steam locomotives, pumps and hydraulic presses. Over the years he devised many improvements in the design and construction of machines and machine tools. These included a flexible shaft for drills, the Nasmyth shaper for planing small surfaces, a double faced wedge form sluice valve (the basis for this type of valve today), a nut milling machine and a portable hand drill.

It was, however, in 1839 that he invented the piece of equipment for which he is chiefly remembered and which was the driving force behind the development of heavy engineering—the steam hammer. The hammer was built as a result of a request from Isambard Kingdom Brunel for the forging of a drive shaft to turn the huge paddle wheels of the projected iron ship, the "Great Britain". In the end, Brunel decided to use screw propellers instead. With its ability to apply tremendous forces under controlled conditions the steam hammer immediately found a whole range of applications in heavy industry. The hammer was so flexible that it could be adjusted to descend with only sufficient power to break an eggshell in a wineglass without breaking the latter. Nasmyth narrowly missed losing the rights to his invention. Initially he did not see the enormous impact of the steam hammer and filed away the drawings in a drawer. In his absence another employee showed Nasmyth's design to Schneider, of the Le Creusot company, and so it was Schneider who actually built the first steam hammer. When Nasmyth saw it in 1841, he learned to his surprise that it was built to his own design; he then, needless to say, lost no time in building and patenting his invention.

James Nasmyth (1808-1890).
ack: National Galleries of Scotland, Edinburgh.

James Nasmyth—painting by him of steam hammer in shed (1871).
ack: Science Museum, London.

The steam hammer was the forerunner of the modern pile driver. With its upright, inverted cylinder, it was also adapted as the basis for a standard design in marine engines. Nasmyth completed the circle of the Industrial Revolution by making it possible for machines to make machines.

From Watt's perfection of the steam engine came generations of engines, designed to meet different applications and to run on different power sources. The Scots played their part in driving industry onwards towards greater and more sophisticated goals. They contributed the Z-crank engine, the two-stroke engine, the oscillating engine, the steeple engine and the Bell-crank engine. Not surprisingly with a tradition of marine engineering the Scots were quick to apply steam power to the design of ships. Innovations include the introduction of the compound engine and the triple expansion engine. It was, however, from a more unexpected source that the heated air engine, which is now attracting renewed attention because of its fuel efficiency, came.

Robert Stirling (1790-1878)

The invention of the hot air engine came not from the laboratory of a Scottish University nor from the drawing board of one of the increasing number of professional engineers but from the pen of a Scottish clergyman, Robert Stirling. His engine provided the key to the development of the open hearth steel furnace, which produced in turn the building blocks of 19th century engineering. It is still used in a number of heat and furnace applications especially in the steel industry.

Stirling designed his prototype hot air engine at the age of twenty-six shortly after moving to his first parish. His engine was the first to incorporate the all important "regenerator", a device which took up heat from the hot air as it flowed one way and gave the heat back to cool air passing in the other direction. It has aptly been described as a "heat sponge" and greatly increased the fuel efficiency of the engine.

Later, Stirling worked with his brother James to improve his engine further; the use of two displacers and pressurised air allowed the engine to cope with greater quantities of heat. One of the first applications of the new engine was in a Dundee foundry where a steam powered beam engine was converted into a Stirling engine. Unfortunately, the engine used to burn out its cylinder bottom every year until in 1847 it was converted back to a steam engine.

A large number of manufacturers in Britain took up and commercially exploited Stirling's invention. The engines were originally used for low power, fixed load duties such as pumping water but their uses increasingly widened to include a number of domestic applications such as portable fans. Because of its thermal efficiency the Stirling engine has created significant interest in the 20th century with companies like Philips researching new applications for Stirling's basic principles.

Hot air engine by **Sir Robert Stirling**.
ack: Science Museum, London.

The SS Great Eastern used in the laying of the Transatlantic Cable 1866.
ack: Science Museum, London.

The "SS Great Eastern", regarded as one of the engineering wonders of the 19th century, links three very different men, all Scots. Without Sir William Fairbairn who pioneered the use of iron for shipbuilding, it might not have been possible. Without John Scott Russell, its builder, it certainly would not have been possible.

When it proved more of a technological wonder than a commercial proposition, it was William Thomson, Lord Kelvin, who gave it a new lease of life as the cable ship for laying the trans-Atlantic submarine cable. These three men, however, have more in common than the "Great Eastern": all three were responsible for advancing engineering knowledge and for creating new specialisms within the profession. Fairbairn was the first true structural engineer, Russell the first naval architect and Kelvin the architect of thermodynamics.

Sir William Fairbairn *(1789-1874)*.

John Scott Russell *(1808-1882)*.
ack: National Galleries of Scotland, Edinburgh.

Sir William Fairbairn *(1789-1874)*

Sir William Fairbairn turned his back on his Scottish origins, as the son of Kelso farm servants, to become one of the great practising engineers of the 19th century. His achievements were wide ranging from the invention of the Lancashire boiler to the building, with Robert Stephenson, of the great Conway and Menai railway bridges. He was the first person to undertake a scientific investigation of the properties of metal as a building material. He was a bridge builder, spanning not only the turbulent waters of the Menai Straits but also the evolution of the engineer from millwright to professional.

As a young man he went to Manchester to set up as a millwright. He not surprisingly first turned his skills to the needs of the local textile industry. He greatly improved the system of driving textile mills by introducing a high speed transmission system using light line shafting running in self-aligning bearings, a system which was to be widely copied by other industries.

He then moved to London to set up a small shipyard in Millwall where he constructed the first iron steamship, the "Lord Dundas". It was there that he was contacted by Robert Stephenson who was in the process of designing the Britannia railway bridge over the Menai Straits. It may seem surprising now but at the time there was little or no theoretical knowledge of the properties of iron as a building material. This was a critical lack as the success of the railways depended as much on the structural engineering involved as on the design of the locomotives. The classic set of experiments conducted by Stephenson and Fairbairn to determine the most suitable form of girder for the Britannia Bridge, laid the foundations of structural engineering as a scientific discipline. The tubular design that they eventually adopted gave rise to another problem, and to another solution devised by Fairbairn. To roll the sections and girders required was beyond the contemporary capabilities of the iron industry and so the tubes were made up of small plates and angles riveted together. In order to handle this volume of work, Fairbairn designed the first riveting machine for metal. The Britannia Bridge had almost twice as long a span as any bridge previously built, but Fairbairn's technique of lattice wrought iron girders was successful and this remained the most popular form of bridge construction until the advent of steel.

Another of Fairbairn's major contributions to the age of steam was his boiler which became the most popular boiler of all time, and is still used today to generate process steam. As the industrial application of the new steam technologies expanded so did the requirement for boilers that could withstand high pressures of steam. By introducing, in 1844, boilers with twin flues and furnaces, firing alternatively, Fairbairn succeeded in his objective of generating a much greater head of steam than the previous Cornish boilers.

In his Presidential address to the British Association at Manchester in 1861, Fairbairn looked both forward and back. He looked back to the days when he *"first entered this city, the whole of the machinery was executed by hand.... Now everything is done by machine tools with a degree of accuracy which the unaided hand could never accomplish"*. Did he also look forward to the days of robotics when he commented that *"the automaton or self-acting machine has within itself an almost creative power"*?

John Scott Russell *(1808-1882)*

The building of the "Great Eastern" has captured the popular imagination as possibly the greatest engineering feat of the 19th century. The builder of what was at the time, by a considerable margin, the world's largest steamship, John Scott Russell has many claims to engineering greatness. He elevated ship design into naval architecture.

He was born in the then weavers' village of Parkhead, soon to be transformed into one of the main engineering centres of Glasgow. He matriculated at the University of Glasgow at the early age of thirteen intending to follow in his father's footsteps as a parish minister. He had a change of heart, however, and it was while teaching mathematics in Edinburgh shortly thereafter that he embarked on his first successful engineering project—the design of a steam carriage. He had always shown an interest in steam power; as a child he had constructed a model steam coach using the family kettle as a boiler. He obtained the backing of a group of Edinburgh businessmen to construct his first vehicle, and after considerable opposition from the Road Trustees finally managed to establish a route between Glasgow and Paisley. His career as a coach proprietor came to a dramatic end in 1834, when one of his coaches crashed with four of the passengers killed. This gives him incidentally the somewhat dubious claim as the originator of the first fatal automobile accident. Litigation followed—the Road Trustees were suspected by some to have put a deliberate obstruction on the road—but Russell's coach business was in ruins.

By this time, Russell's interests were turning to shipbuilding and in particular to hydrodynamics, a subject which at the time was little studied. He built three experimental wave-line vessels for the Union Canal Company, and it was on the Union Canal that he made his discovery of the phenomenon of the soliton or single wave in 1834. He immediately realised the significance of his observation and pursued the solitary wave for several miles on horseback. It was not, however, for many years after his death that scientists realised the full potential of the soliton in its application to radar, computer and optical fibre technologies.

He used his observations on the solitary wave of translation to redesign the shape of ships' bows. His subsequent studies of the design of ships' hulls, in relation to the water that they travelled through, gave shipbuilders their first scientific guide in their pursuit of speed. In 1838, Russell himself entered the shipbuilding industry as manager of a Greenock yard where he produced his first wave-line designs for ships destined for open waters.

In 1844, he moved south to take up a completely new career as a journalist on Sir Charles Dilke's "Railway Chronicle". He later also served as Railway Editor on Charles Dicken's newspaper, the "Daily News". In 1847, however, he was enticed back to the sea, or at least the dockside, by an offer from a new shipbuilding firm who had taken over Sir William Fairbairn's yard at Millwall. Ship design was combined over the next few years with a heavy involvement in the planning and organisation of the first World Fair, the Great Exhibition of 1851. It was also during this period that he evolved his designs of iron ships to include longitudinal bracing.

In 1852, Russell entered discussions with Isambard Kingdom Brunel on a project to build the world's largest steamship. The whole conception was staggering in both size and complexity but Russell painstakingly drew and redrew the designs for this mammoth enterprise. After many vicissitudes including near bankruptcy and an increasingly strained relationship with the ebullient and wayward Brunel, Russell held a party on board the "Great Eastern" to celebrate the completion of its building in 1856. On its first sea trials, however, the forward funnel exploded and it was not finally until 1860 that she made her maiden voyage. Brunel took most of the credit at the time but Russell's abilities as designer and shipbuilder are now seen as outstanding. He tackled and overcame the unprecedented problems posed by the gigantic size of the "Great Eastern" and its novel structure.

Russell continued as a shipbuilder for the rest of his career, specialising in naval warships. His latter years were taken up increasingly with the problems of running several major engineering businesses. Financial speculation and business management came less naturally to him than the design of a hull or the shape of a wave as it broke on the bows. Russell's life might have been even more fruitful and certainly less fraught with anxieties if, like James Watt, he had found his Matthew Boulton.

William Thomson, Lord Kelvin *(1824-1907)*

Kelvin started out in life in the way that he continued to the end of his days. He was a true infant prodigy attending his father's mathematics lectures with delight at the age of eight. During his teens he wrote a mathematical paper that was read to the Royal Society of Edinburgh. The reader, however, was an elderly professor as it was considered undignified for such an august body to be lectured to by a child.

From the age of twenty three, Kelvin held the Chair of Natural Philosophy at the University of Glasgow and was one of the first to teach physics in the laboratory as well as in the lecture hall. His interests as a young man lay primarily in the study of heat. An early supporter of Joule, he collaborated with him to work out what has become known as the Joule-Thomson effect, involving the manner in which gases undergo a drop in temperature when they expand into a vacuum. This research proved crucial a generation later to the work of James Dewar's liquefaction of gases and obtaining of ultra-low temperatures.

Lord Kelvin *(1824-1907)* lecturing.
ack: the Department of Natural Philosophy, University of Glasgow.

43

The Engineering Giants

In 1848 Kelvin estimated the point of absolute zero to be – 273 degrees C remarkably close to the modern calculation. He proposed a new scale of temperature with its base at absolute zero and its degrees equal to those on the Centigrade scale. This scale is known in honour of Kelvin as the Kelvin scale. The scale was quickly adopted and fellow Scot, William Rankine adapted it for use by engineers. The absolute temperature scale of degrees Fahrenheit is known as the Rankine scale.

In 1851 Kelvin deduced the proposition that all energy tends to dissipate itself as heat, a form of the second law of thermodynamics. It was also Kelvin who introduced the terms "kinetic energy" and "potential" to the vocabulary of science. He developed the wave theory of light and the study of molecular dynamics.

He was by no means simply an academic scientist. He became interested in the proposed project to lay a telegraph cable across the Atlantic and his studies of the capacity of a cable to carry an electric signal led to his improvements to cables and galvanometer without which the laying of the cable would have proved useless. He was a Director of the Atlantic Telegraph Company and of the Kodak company. He himself undertook the manufacture of several of his inventions in the area of scientific instrumentation and made significant improvements to the mariner's compass. In 1881 he put forward a proposal to harness the energy of the Niagara Falls into hydro-electricity and was the first person to put forward the concept of the heat pump.

He was also one of the great all rounders. He was a keen rower, winning the Colquhoun silver sculls, and later founded the Glasgow University Musical Society. He was an enthusiast for the innovations of others: his house was the first in Scotland to be lit by electricity and he introduced the Bell telephone to the UK. Sadly in his old age Kelvin's ideas became more fixed: he is reported to have said that all the discoveries in physics had been made and all that remained to do was to adjust the decimal point in a number of measurements. With almost his dying breath he denounced the first evidence that physics was to be turned on its head again, when he bitterly opposed the idea that radioactive atoms were disintegrating or that the energy released came from within the atom.

Kelvin was the architect of 19th century physics: his building complete, he rested rather than turn to the next new design.

The fact that the "Great Eastern" reached graceful retirement as a showboat on the Mersey rather than sink to the bottom of the Atlantic can be credited partly to the rather more unusual contribution of one of Scotland's engineering families.

The Stevenson Family

"But I, when I am stronger
And can choose what I'm to do
Oh, Leerie, I'll go round at night
And light the lamps with you."

Robert Louis Stevenson was not the only member of his family to want to be a lamp lighter when he grew up. The rest of his family, however, were interested in providing a guiding light for ships rather than pedestrians.

From 1800 to 1938, the Stevenson family acted as engineers to the Northern Lighthouse Board and by their innovative contribution made the sea a much safer place for shipping. This was a crucial contribution in an age when sea was the only means of transporting people and cargo to other parts of the world and when navigators did not have the modern technologies of radar and radio to guide them.

The first of the "lighthouse" Stevensons was **Robert** (1772-1850). Robert was originally destined for the ministry, but his fortunes changed when his widowed mother married one Thomas Smith, engineer to the newly established Northern Lighthouse Board. He became an apprentice to his stepfather, studying at Glasgow and then Edinburgh Universities in the winter months when lighthouse work was not possible. Despite studying for twelve years, he never graduated, attributing this to *"my slender knowledge of Latin and my total want of Greek"*.

In 1800 he set out on his major task, the erection of the Bell Rock Lighthouse on the much feared reef twelve miles out into the stormy North Sea from Arbroath. Its successful completion made Stevenson a national figure. He invented a number of modifications to lighthouses including flashing and intermittent lights and an instrument for taking samples of water at given depths. He was the first person to observe that salt water from the ocean flows up a river in a distinct stream from the fresh water flowing down. He also gave his namesake, George Stephenson the idea of malleable iron rails on which to run his steam engines.

Whereas Robert Stevenson was something of a pioneer and a jack of all trades in lighthouse engineering, his three sons, Alan, David and Thomas, who followed in his footsteps were able to refine his techniques and to conduct original research in areas such as lighthouse optics and meteorology. **David Stevenson** introduced paraffin lighting in lighthouses which allowed a much more intense light. Among his commissions, were several in Japan where he devised an aseismatic version to counteract the effect of earthquakes. **Thomas Stevenson,** father of the poet

Robert Stevenson (1772-1850).
ack: National Galleries of Scotland, Edinburgh.

The Bell Rock Lighthouse built 1800 twelve miles out in the North Sea off Arbroath.
ack: Arbroath Museum, Angus.

and essayist, developed the aximurthal condensing system for lighthouses and the Stevenson screen for thermometers.

It was Robert's grandson **Charles Stevenson** (1855-1950) who realised the potential of the technologies that were dawning. On a trip to America, he saw a demonstration of the newly invented Bell telephone. It inspired his imagination, and he spent the next fifteen years striving to find a means of transmitting speech across distance without wires, in order to be able to maintain better communications with isolated lighthouses.

He managed to solve the problem in principle two years before Marconi started his famous experiments; but his employers, although appreciative of the potential of his invention, were unable to find the finance for practical trials. His work was soon overtaken by Marconi's spectacular success. In later life, he adapted radio to devise his "Talking Beacon" which enabled ships to plot their course in fog by means of synchronised radio and fog signals.

The 19th century was the great age of steam. One of the Scottish engineers who carried the tradition over into the twentieth century was Sir Dugald Clerk. In his invention of the two-stroke engine, he saw himself as simply applying Kelvin's formulation of the second law of thermodynamics, or indeed continuing to supply the life and soul of science. His two-stroke engine, however, was the progenitor of the modern motor cycle engine.

Sir Dugald Clerk (1854-1932)

Sir Dugald Clerk put Kelvin's principles into practice. Much of his work was based on Kelvin's development of the second law of thermodynamics. When in his last years, Clerk met with a younger man who cast some doubts on the validity of the law, he dismissed his critic with the words *"Why man, I've made my living off it"*.

A successful living it was too. Clerk who was brought up and educated in Glasgow, rose to become the Director of Research at the Admiralty after a career in several engineering firms and as senior partner in a large firm of patent agents.

Clerk had been a keen follower of recent developments in engine design on the Continent, notably the Otto four-stroke engine. He reasoned that it would be possible to produce an engine with a power stroke in every revolution. Applying scientific principles to explain and to design the thermodynamic cycle of the ICE, Clerk built the first two-stroke engine in 1879. He used two equal sized cylinders. One cylinder sucked in and compressed the mixture feeding it to a reservoir from which it passed to the power cylinder. When the piston in the power cylinder began its outward travel, the mixture was admitted through a slide valve. On its inward stroke, the power piston exhausted the spent gas through a poppet-valve. In 1881 the engine was further modified to use a much lower charging pressure.

Clerk's two-stroke engine formed the basis for many applications including the motor cycle and the lawnmower. The principles that he established are still used today in the design of large gas engines.

Today the Scottish engineering industry continues on its innovative path. The industry itself is changing rapidly. Now the demand is not for ships that go faster or for great feats of steelwork like the Forth Railway Bridge. Today's demand is more for electronic transmission and motorway interchanges. The Scots were in at the beginning of these too with James Clerk Maxwell and Andrew Thomson, the father of the box girder. In a small workshop outside Glasgow or in the laboratory of Strathclyde University, the oldest technological institution of its kind, the engineering innovations of the 21st century may now be on the drawing board.

Thomas Stevenson
ack: National Galleries of Scotland, Edinburgh.

Sir Dugald Clerk (1854-1932).
ack: National Galleries of Scotland, Edinburgh.

The Engineering Giants

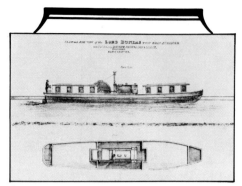

The 'Lord Dundas' first iron steamship 1831 litho by
H G James.
ack: The National Maritime Museum, London.

The 'Cutty Sark' the record-breaking tea clipper,
built on the Clyde (1869).
Photo taken by her master, Captain Woodgit.
ack: The National Maritime Museum, London.

Scots achievements in shipbuilding

The first paddle wheel steamer: "Charlotte Dundas" built by **William Symington**. *1802.*

The Brown-Curtis marine turbine: designed by **Sir John Biles** for **J and G Thomson** of Clydebank.

The introduction of the triple expansion engine to marine engineering: **John Elder and Company**, Glasgow "Propontis". *1880.*

Corrugated marine flues: **John Scott**. *1830-1903.*

The water tube boiler: **Yarrows**. *1894.*

The first merchant ship to be powered by steam turbines: "King Edward". *1904.*

The first all steel shipping vessel: Clyde pleasure steamer built by **William Denny and Brothers**. *1876.*

The first iron steamship: "Lord Dundas", built by **Sir William Fairbairn**. *1789-1874.*

The first ocean going all steel vessel: **William Denny and Brothers**. *1879.*

The first paddle steamer to cross the Atlantic: "Sirius" *1838.*

The first steamboat to cross the Channel: built by **William Denny and Brothers**.

The first steam whaler: built in Dundee. *1857.*

The first ship to cross the Atlantic in less than a week: "Alaska", built on the Clyde by **John Elder and Company**. *1881.*

The fastest clipper of all time : "Mailesden", built in Dundee.

The first iron passenger boat: built in Airdrie. *1819.*

The first stern trawler: "Fairtry" built by **J Lewis and Sons Limited**, Aberdeen in *1954.*

The first steel built mail steamer to cross the Atlantic: "Parisian" built by **Robert Napier and Sons**. *1881.*

The first "Atlantic Greyhound": "Arizona" built on the Clyde by **J Elder and Company**. *1879.*

The first merchant steamer to sail through the Magellan Straits: "Zeta" built by **Alexander Stephen**. *1865.*

The first turbine powered passenger ship to cross the Atlantic: "Virginian", built by **Alexander Stephen**. *1905.*

The first steel ship to cross the Atlantic: "Buenos Aires", built by **William Denny and Brothers**. *1887.*

The record breaking tea clipper: "Cutty Sark", built by **Scott and Linton**, Dumbarton. *1869.*

The first set of triple expansion engines for a twin screw steamer: designed by **Rankine and Blackmore** of Greenock.

The first merchant ship adapted to run on oil: launched from **John Brown and Company Limited.** Clydebank. *1913.*

The McLaggan Diesel Engine: designed by **John McLaggan.** *1886-1962.*

The paddle wheel: patented by **Patrick Miller.** *In the 1780's.*

The first seagoing, heavy-oil motor ship: designed by **The Duke of Montrose.** *1878-1954.*

The slipway: invented by **Thomas Morton.** *1781-1832.*

The use of surface condensation in marine engines: **David Napier.** *1790-1869.*

The tubular marine boiler: **John Napier.** *1830.*

The wave line system of construction in ships: **John Scott Russell.** *1808-82.*

Longitudinal bracing in ships: **John Scott Russell.** *1808-82.*

Jet propulsion in shipping: **J. Ruthven.** *1839.*

Lead electric cables in ships: introduced by **Archibald Campbell Swinton.** *1863-1930.*

The germinal steamboat: **William Symington.** *1762-1831.*

The ship's stabiliser: **Sir William Wallace.** b. *1881.*

The design of ships' hulls for steam propulsion: **John and Charles Wood.** *1820's.*

The first ship to be fitted with two engines: "Princess Charlotte". *1814.*

The first ship to cross the Atlantic under continuous steam: "Sirius", built in Leith. *1838.*

The first power vessel to cross the Atlantic: "Curacao", built in Dundee. *1827.*

The first ocean going ship to be fitted with a surface condenser: "Sirius". *1838.*

The first motor ship built in the UK: "Jutlandia" built by **Barclay Curle and Company,** Glasgow for East Asiatic Company Copenhagen.

The first commercially successful steamship in Europe: "Comet", built for **Henry Bell** by **John Wood,** Shipbuilder, Port Glasgow. *1812.*

The servo-motor for the hydraulic steering of ships: **D B Brown.** *1870.*

The use of test tanks in shipbuilding design: **William Denny and Brothers.**

The first passenger steamer powered by steam turbines: "King Edward" built by **William Denny and Brothers.** Dumbarton. *1901.*

The first steam tug in Europe: "Samson", built by **William Denny and Brothers.**

The first all-welded ship: **William Denny and Brothers.**

The idea of variable speed trials for ships: **William Denny and Brothers.**

The first ocean going ship with compound engines: "Brandon" built by **John Elder** and **Charles Randolph** on the Clyde in *1854.* (Randolph, Elder and Company).

This illustration of the 'Alaska' in the Mersey does full justice to the long, low and balanced profile of a Blue Riband holder which served the Guion Line to the end. She is chiefly remembered as being the first vessel to make the Atlantic crossing in under a week.
ack: Richard Dell, Strathclyde Regional Archives, Glasgow.

The first commercially successful steamship in Europe, the 'Comet', built by Henry Bell, in *1812.* Photo shows the 'Comet' passing Dumbarton Rock on the Clyde *1815.*
ack: the Graham Collection, Glasgow Room, Mitchell Library, Glasgow.

Scottish achievements in engineering

The Lancashire boiler: **Sir William Fairbairn.** *1789-1874.*
Comminuting plant (to crush fruit for fruit squash): **Edward Hamilton.** *1854.*
Machine for extruding spaghetti.
The first commercial refrigeration plant in the UK: built for a Bathgate paraffin refiner. *1861.*
The first textile machinery driven by steam: designed in *1785* by **James Watt.** *1736-1819.*
Power setting loom for weaving Axminster carpets: **William Adam.** *1882.*
Diamond tipped circular saw for stone cutting: **George Anderson.** *1880's.*
Machine for granulating gunpowder: **Sir John Anderson.** *1814-86.*
The hydraulic spade and the hydraulic riveter: **Sir William Arrol.** *1839-1913.*
The first steam driven power loom: **Austin** of Glasgow. *1789.*
Multi-tubular and water-tube boilers: pioneered on the Clyde. *1880's.*
The barrel and the 3-ply carpet loom: **Thomas Morton** and **Andrew Barclay.** *1820's.*
The cam-operated weaving loom: **William Bell.** *1794.*
The cylindrical roller for cotton printing: **Thomas Bell.** *1783.*
The machine to produce variable pitch mesh: **Alexander Buchan.** *1830.*
The spindle type of cotton picking machinery: **Angus Campbell.** *1889.*
The two-stroke engine: **Sir Dugald Clerk.** *1854-1932.*
The converter-coupling for use in vehicle automatic transmission: **Allan Coats.** *1924.*
The water cooled tuyère in metal processing: **John Condie.** *1830.*
Sawing machine to cut veneer: **Alexander Craig.** *1824.*
Mechanical ice-making machine: **William Cullen.** *1710-90.*
The tank engine: **Sir William Fairbairn.** *1789-1874.*
The machine for the weaving of long haired silk: **Gibson** and **Campbell.** *1836.*
The practical heat pump: **Thomas Haldane.** *b. 1897.*
The perfection of the bobbin and fly frame for twisting cotton: **Henry Houldsworth.** *1825.*
The development of forced draught technology in boiler design: **James Howden.**
The first riveting machine for metal: **Sir William Fairbairn.** *1789-1874.*
The steam turbine: **David Justice.**
Power loom for cotton weaving: **William Kelly.** *1792.*
Zigzag winding for alternators: **Lord Kelvin.** *1824-1907.*
The sack sewing machine: **James Laing.** *1880's.*
Hinge shutters and the fantail gear for windmills: **Andrew Meikle.** *1719-1811.*
The change shuttle allowing the introduction of powered multi-colour weaving: **Mitchell and Whytlaw Limited.** *1850.*
The Z crank engine: **Morton** and **Hunt.** *1855.*
The sun and planet wheel: **William Murdoch.** *1754-1839.*
The planing machine for floorboards: **Malcolm Muir.** *1827.*
The revolution counter: **James Watt.** *1736-1819.*
The slide valve: **William Murdoch.** *1754-1839.*
The steeple engine: **David Napier.** *1790-1869.*
The fishtail gas burner: **James Neilson.** *1792-1865.*
The bell crank engine: **William Murdoch.** *1754-1839.*
The continuous rotary printing machine: **Thomas Nelson.** *c. 1850.*
The first machine to make fishing nets: **James Paterson.** *c. 1770-1840.*
The evaporator: **The Weir Group.**
The eccentric: **William Murdoch.** *1754-1839.*
The dog clutch: **John Rennie.** *1761-1821.*
The oscillating engine: **William Murdoch.** *1754-1839.*
The continuous action sugar drying machine: **David Napier.** *1790-1869.*
The first all iron manufacturing plant: **John Rennie.** *1761-1821.*
Desalination plant: **Robert Silver.** *b. 1913.*
Radial and axial flow for steam turbines: **Robert Wilson.** *1803-82.*
The modern lighthouse: **The Stevenson Family.**
Vertical casting of iron pipes: **D Y Stewart.** *1840.*
The heated air engine: **Robert Stirling.** *1790-1878.*
The vortex turbine: **James Thomson.** *1850.*
The rotary exhauster: **Robert Thomson.** *1822-75.*
The separate condenser: **James Watt.** *1736-1819.*
The direct acting feed pump: **The Weir Group.**
The ejector water pump: **James Thomson.** *1852.*
The double acting engine: **James Watt.** *1736-1819.*
The centrifugal governor: **James Watt.** *1736-1819.*
Feedwater heating in boilers: **The Weir Group.** *1880.*
The hydrokimeter: **The Weir Group.** *1874.*
The Scotch mill, arguably the first turbine: **James Whitelaw.** *1839.*
The practical screw propeller: **Robert Wilson.** *1803-82.*

Making the World Go Faster

HENRY BELL

*"The Clyde made Glasgow and
Glasgow made the Clyde"*
Anon

Making the World Go Faster

The mode of travel that is most associated with Scotland and especially with the Clyde is, of course, the ship. If one thinks of speed, one thinks of the "Cutty Sark", built on the Clyde in 1869: if one thinks of majesty, one thinks of the Queens, launched on the Clyde in the 1930's. Warships like "HMS Hood" and "Renown", Blue Riband holders, giant tankers, Empresses and Princesses all made their stately way down the Clyde at the start of their maritime careers.

With Scotland's natural resources and skills in engineering, backed by the academic knowledge of the first Department of Naval Architecture in the world, it is perhaps not surprising that the Scottish yards were responsible for many marine innovations from the first practical screw propeller to the compound marine engine. They adapted the ingenuity and expertise of Scots in other branches of the engineer's art to the building of great ships.

Warship: HMS Renown, built on the Clyde.
ack: Richard Dell, Strathclyde Regional Archives, Glasgow.

"THE QUEENS"
Queen Elizabeth and Queen Mary in Southampton Harbour.
ack: Southern Newspapers, PLC, Southampton.

William Symington
designed the first practical steamboat.
ack: The Scottish Maritime Museum, Irvine.

The origins of the application of steam to navigation, however, lie far from the great shipyards of the Clyde.

William Symington *(1762-1831)*

Symington was a pioneer in the application of steam to water navigation. He designed the first practical steam boat in the UK, under commission from the landowner, eccentric and amateur technologist, Patrick Miller of Dalswinton near Dumfries. The steamboat, which appears to have been nameless, was twenty five foot long and capable of a speed of about five miles per hour. Symington's atmospheric, twin-cylinder engine drove two paddle-wheels, set one behind the other, between the hulls of the catamaran-type boat.

On the first test run of the boat on Dalswinton Loch in 1788, Symington and Miller's fellow passengers were James Taylor, tutor to the Miller children, Alexander Nasmyth, the portrait painter and the poet, Robert Burns who was a tenant on the estate. According to Taylor, the steamboat *"answered Mr Miller's expectation fully and afforded great pleasure to the spectators present"*.

The first steamship in the world on Dalswinton Loch at 5 mph in October, 1788.
ack: The Scottish Maritime Museum, Irvine.

Symington went on to design the first steamboat using a piston rod coupled to a crankshaft by a connecting rod, a design that has been standard ever since. He was commissioned on this occasion by Lord Dundas who planned to use it on the Forth and Clyde Canal. The fifty six foot long boat, christened the "Charlotte Dundas", was propelled by a stern paddle wheel. During her trials in 1801, she proved capable of towing two barges of seventy tons along a nineteen and a half mile stretch of the Canal. Despite her initial success, however, she was soon abandoned, as it was feared that her wash would damage the canal banks. As she lay idle, she was the subject of a visit by Robert Fulton, the Scots descended American designer of the world's first commercial steam boat, and Henry Bell whose "Comet", launched on the Clyde in 1812, was to become the first commercially successful steamboat in Europe. Symington provided the inspiration for over a century of steam.

Robert Fulton's first commercial steamboat 'Clermont', sometimes called 'North River'.
ack: The National Maritime Museum, London.

Model of the "Charlotte Dundas".
ack: The Scottish Maritime Museum, Irvine.

'The Comet' (launched on the Clyde 1812).
ack: The Scottish Maritime Museum, Irvine.

The Scots have also made some rather more unexpected contributions to modern transport. The motorway lanes of today owe their speed and smoothness to the man who gave his name to tarmac.

John Loudon McAdam *(1756-1836)*

Ayrshire born and bred, McAdam emigrated to New York as a young man to work for his uncle who was a staunch Tory. He adopted his uncle's politics and so the Declaration of Independence saw an end to his career in the now United States.

It was in 1806 on his appointment as paving commissioner in Bristol that McAdam "paved the way" for his name to become a household word. He began to campaign energetically for the adoption of new and efficient ways of road surfacing. He suggested making roads out of crushed rock with proper drainage rather than the ruts or mud of the existing untreated carriageways. His road

John McAdam *(1756-1836)*.
His principles of roadmaking are still in essence used in motorways today.
ack: National Galleries of Scotland, Edinburgh.

John McAdam's first road on his estate near Sauchie, still in use today.
ack: National Trust for Scotland.

Making the World Go Faster

making system involved the use of graded stones, laying the largest size of about two inches diameter on the soil to a depth of six inches and building up towards the surface with layers of stones of decreasing size. It is estimated that by the end of the 19th century ninety per cent of European roads were "macadamised" and his principles of roadmaking are still, in essence, used in the motorways of today. McAdam was catering for the age of the stage coach: his invention is equally applicable to the age of the motor car.

Pedalling perhaps along a macadamised road or more likely a rutted country lane came the world's first cyclist.

Kirkpatrick MacMillan *(1813-1878)*

The son of a Dumfriesshire blacksmith, MacMillan followed in his father's footsteps. In 1837, he built himself a "dandy horse" a contraption somewhat like a bicycle but which was propelled by pushing on the ground with one's feet. From this, he conceived the idea of propelling the machine by a crank activated by pedals and built the world's first pedal cycle.

His first machine, built in 1839, weighed fifty seven pounds and was propelled by a crank on the rear wheel coupled to two horizontal pedal levers which oscillated back and forwards. The frame of the bicycle was of wood with a carved horse's head on the front: the wheels had iron tyres.

MacMillan did not recognise the great commercial potential of his personal transport revolution. He saw it solely as an efficient means of getting about, often travelling the fourteen miles from his home to Dumfries on it. In 1842 he ventured as far as Glasgow taking an evening and part of a day to complete the 70 mile journey. This journey provided him unwittingly with another claim to immortality as the first person to commit a cycling offence. He accidentally knocked over a child in the crush of people who had come out to see his novel "iron horse" and was fined five shillings at Gorbals Police Court.

In the early 1840's his niece, Mary Marchbank, took to riding his machine and thus became the world's first lady cyclist.

It was for his children's bicycle that John Boyd Dunlop, a Scots born vet in Belfast, first designed the pneumatic tyre. The commercial development of his invention nearly foundered on the discovery that he had not in fact invented the

tyre but simply reinvented it. A patent for an india rubber tyre had been taken out in 1845 by one of the most remarkable of Scottish inventors of the 19th century.

R W Thomson *(1822-73)*

Thomson's contribution to making the world go faster was the pneumatic tyre, only one of the many innovations from his fertile mind. The son of a Stonehaven merchant, he was originally destined for the Church. A lack of aptitude for academic study however persuaded his father to pack him off instead to Charleston in the United States to train as a merchant.

Thomson soon returned to his native land. It was while working for his cousin on the demolition of Dunbar Castle that he made his first contribution to innovation—the use of electricity for firing mines. In 1841 he headed south for London where his ideas on electricity were taken up by no less an expert than Michael Faraday. He was employed for a time by William Cubitt on his blasting operations on Dover cliffs.

Thomson believed in gaining varied experience. After a spell as a civil engineer in Glasgow, a railway engineer under Robert Stephenson and a railway agent on his own account, he took up employment as an engineering agent in Java. By then

Kirkpatrick MacMillan *(1813-1878).*
ack: Museum of Transport, Glasgow.

Contemporary copy of Kirkpatrick MacMillan's pedal cycle—the first pedal cycle.
ack: Museum of Transport, Glasgow.

Robert Thomson *(1822-1873).*
ack: National Galleries of Scotland, Edinburgh.

he had invented his pneumatic tyre, which he patented in 1845. His tyres were of leather with inner tubes of rubberised canvas and were fitted on to a horse drawn brougham. Owing to the price of rubber at the time, however, the tyres were not a commercial proposition and their widespread use had to wait for John Boyd Dunlop. In 1849 Thomson patented the first self-acting fountain pen which had a reservoir for storing ink: this, in many ways, was the precursor of the modern fountain pen. Its ingenuity won it a place in the Great Exhibition of 1851.

While in Java, Thomson turned his mind to improving the machinery in use in the sugar plantations. He wished to erect a crane on the waterside as part of this project but the authorities insisted that it would have to be dismantled every night in case the inhabitants fell over it. Undaunted, Thomson set his mind to solving this problem and came up with the first portable steam crane.

In 1862, he retired to Edinburgh but his inventive mind did not retire. There was a need to be able to move traction engines round the sugar plantations in Java. Thomson came up trumps again. He designed the first successful, mechanically propelled vehicles for road haulage over long distances. His first two steam tractors, "Chenab" and "Ravee", were built in 1871 by Ransome, Sims and Head of Ipswich for Lt. R E B Crompton's Government Steam Train. The "Ravee" was test run between Ipswich and Edinburgh and then the vehicles, along with one to a similar design called the "Indus", were shipped out in parts to Rawalpindi and assembled for use by the Indian Transport Service. The steamers were put into service, carrying both passengers and freight over a seventy mile stretch of the Grand Trunk Road between Jhelum and Rawalpindi. Refuelling stations were set up at fourteen mile intervals along the route with water tanks every seven miles. The "trains" ran at an average speed of five to eight miles per hour. Freight capacity was considerable. The "Indus" drew a load of 64.3 tons up a gradient of 1:33 during a test run: the main limitation was a shortage of suitable rolling stock. They had huge tyres like elephant's pads to spread the load of the traction engines.

The "steamers", as they were nicknamed, came into their own in parts of the world where, either due to the roughness of the terrain or lack of capital, there were no railways. One firm, Robey's of Lincoln, alone made sixty such vehicles in the period 1871-91. They were also used in the UK, although usually over shorter distances. Captain Losada, Manager of the Glasgow Tramways claimed that Thomson steamers were considered of such value in Glasgow that *"no single article weighing over ten tons is ever moved except by one of them"*.

Thomson's pneumatic tyre (replica).
ack: Science Museum, London.

Thomson Road Steamer at Port of Glasgow.
ack: Museum of Transport, Glasgow.

Sir Keith Elphinstone (1864-1944).
ack: National Portrait Gallery, London.

With smooth roads and smooth tyres, there may be a temptation for the motorist to travel too fast. The means of making sure that his journey does not end at the police station was given to the motorist by Sir Keith Elphinstone with the speedometer.

Sir Keith Elphinstone (1864-1944)

Coming from an aristocratic and naval family, Keith Elphinstone's first love was the sea. A childhood illness, however, left him lame and so he turned to industry for a career.

On leaving school he bought a company in London and spent his next few years engaged in installing some of the earliest privately owned electric light and telephone equipment. He then joined the electrical and mechanical engineering firm, Elliott Brothers, with whom he remained for the rest of his career, rising to become Chairman.

In the period up to the outbreak of the First World War his name was associated with the invention of many electrical and mechanical devices. His was the first British firm to manufacture micrometers and he invented the continuous roll chart recorder. His association with motor speed is twofold. He designed and installed the original speed recording system at the race track at Brooklands where so many of the early motor racing records were established. He also gave the ordinary motorist the speedometer.

The outbreak of war, however, brought Elphinstone closer to his real ambition and he spent the rest of his career designing instruments for the Admiralty including the development of fire-control tables and the production of gunfire control equipment.

The Scots even took to the air, and provided Britain with its first aeronaut. Tytler's story, however, is not entirely a happy one.

James Tytler (1745-1804)

Tytler, undoubtedly a "lad o' pairts" and not all of them good, earns his place in the history of aviation in Britain as the first man in the air.

He was born in a small village in Angus, the fourth child of the local minister. After serving his apprenticeship to a surgeon he moved to Edinburgh to study medicine. Due to financial constraints which were tightened further by an early marriage, Tytler was forced to abandon his studies for more lucrative pursuits. Not that he was very successful. His varied career included chemist, surgeon, printer, poet, textbook writer, journalist, apothecary and political agitator. Eventually his wife despaired of his financial ventures and left him, bequeathing him the care of their five children.

His mainstay over the next seven years was the editorship of the second edition of the Encyclopaedia Britannica, to which he contributed 9000 pages. This, however, did not improve his financial circumstances as he was paid the subsistence wage for a single man. It was this work and the need for money that inspired him to his aeronautical adventures.

He eagerly followed the exploits of the French balloonists, the Montgolfier Brothers, and incorporated eight pages on ballooning in his appendix to the Encyclopaedia. He also saw the money-spinning potential of such an exploit and in 1784 constructed a model balloon, "the Grand Edinburgh Fire Balloon" which he exhibited to the public for the payment of a sixpenny admission charge.

The response fired him with enthusiasm to build a real balloon. He was constantly hampered by lack of resources and his first few attempts, widely advertised in order to raise money, ended in disaster. Finally on the morning of Friday 27 August 1784, before an increasingly restless and jeering crowd, he was successful. He reached a height of 350 feet before drifting gradually to land about half a mile north of his starting point. It was in this way that Tytler became not only Britain's first aeronaut but also her first aeronautical engineer, having designed, built and successfully flown his hot air balloon.

Sadly, however, Tytler's subsequent career continued on its unsuccessful course. Buoyed by his brief success, he made three further balloon attempts in 1784, all of which proved a complete fiasco. He then turned to the role of agitator in favour of political reform and only succeeded in getting arrested for seditious libel. Before his case could be brought to court, he had fled to Ireland and then to Massachusetts to start a new life. The new life, however, proved illusory and he had soon acquired, as well as a third wife and twin daughters, a long record of business failures. He increasingly took to drowning his sorrows and this led in turn to his own watery end in a creek at Salem in 1804.

Fowls of a Feather Flock together.

James Tytler (1745-1804).
Third from left. The first manned flight in the UK was a balloon ascent by him in 1784.
From John Kay's Original Portraits and Etchings.
ack: Mitchell Library, Glasgow.

The Flying Scotsman

The aerostatic principle of the balloon was first demonstrated by **Joseph Black:** *1728-99.*

It is claimed that **P Watson** of Blairgowrie made a successful flight in a heavier than air machine in *1903*, before the Wright Brothers made their historic flight.

The first manned flight in the UK was a balloon ascent by the Edinburgh "Jack of All Trades" **James Tytler** in *1784.*

It was a Scot, **Don Cameron,** who made the first Atlantic crossing in a hot air balloon: *1978.*

Neil Armstrong, the first man to walk on the moon, **John Glenn,** the first US astronaut, and **Bruce McCandless,** the first person to walk in space untethered, are all of Scots descent.

Arthur Whitten Brown who with Alcock undertook the first non-stop Atlantic flight in *1919*, was born in Glasgow of American parents.

Neil Armstrong being made first freeman of Langholm in 1972 (Langholm is a centre of the Armstrong country).
ack: Glasgow Herald and Evening Times.

Alan Bean, the US astronaut, wore a piece of the McBean tartan on his space suit when he stepped on the moon, to commemorate his Scots ancestry.

The first East West solo flight across the Atlantic was made by **James Mollison** in *1931.*

The **14th Duke of Hamilton** was the first person to fly over Mount Everest, in *1933.*

The first trans-Atlantic airship flight set off from East Fortune aerodrome.

The first helicopter (capable of lifting a man off the ground) was built by the Clyde engineers, **William Denny and Brothers.**

The first fully controllable helicopter was built by the Glasgow engineers, **The Weir Group.**

The first airship to cross the Atlantic both ways was built in Clydebank.

The basis for the production of maps of air travel was designed by **John Bartholomew** in *1849.*

The combustion system for Sir Frank Whittle's jet engine was designed by the Scottish company, **Laidlaw Drew:** *1930's.*

The first controlled glider flight in the U.K. was made by **P S Pilcher,** a lecturer at Glasgow University at the turn of the century.

The autorotative principle in helicopter design was evolved by the Glasgow engineering company, **The Weir Group.**

Scots firsts on wheels

The Brougham: designed by and named after the Edinburgh born **Henry, Lord Brougham** in *1838.*

The steam tricycle: designed and ridden by **Andrew Lawson,** an Aberdeenshire postman in *1895.* It was nicknamed the Craigievar Express.

Arthur Whitten Brown (who with Alcock undertook the first non-stop Atlantic flight in 1919) was born in Glasgow of American parents.
ack: BBC Hulton Picture Library, London.

12 H.P. ARGYLL (Four - Cylinder)

R.A.C., 12·8 H.P.   Tax, 4 Guineas

The first motor cars with four-wheel brakes: designed and manufactured in Scotland around 1910.
ack: Museum of Transport, Glasgow.

The first electric locomotive in the UK, designed by Robert Davidson in *1842*.
ack: Department of Science and Technology, Mitchell Library, Glasgow.

The Diesel Electric Rail Motor Train—the first British diesel-electric train was adapted by the London, Midland and Scottish Railway in 1928 from an ex-Lancashire and Yorkshire Railway Manchester-Bury electric train, by fitting it with a 500 hp Beardmore engine and English Electric traction equipment. It ran for a time on the Preston-Blackpool service and was later reconverted to an electric train.
ack: Department of Science and Technology, Mitchell Library, Glasgow.

First motor car with four-wheel brakes: the 11 h.p. **Arrol Johnston** designed and manufactured in Scotland in *1909*.

The train ferry: the world's first passenger train ferry opened in *1850*, crossed the Forth.

The motor bus: a three wheeled steam motor bus designed by **Andrew Nairn** of Leith in *1869*.

The railway excursion train: first organised by the Garnkirk and Glasgow Railway in *1834*.

The motor lorry: the first was built by **John Yule** of Glasgow in *1870* to transport marine boilers.

The diesel engined lorry: the first in the UK was designed by a Glasgow firm in *1927*.

The railway sleeper: the first in the UK was built in Glasgow in *1873* for service on the Glasgow-London route.

The diesel electric locomotive: the first in the UK was built in Glasgow in *1928*.

The cable underground railway: the first was the Glasgow Underground.

The electric locomotive: the first in the UK was designed by **Thomas Davidson** in *1842*.

The pneumatic tyre: invented in *1845* by **Robert Thomson** *1822-73*: reinvented by fellow Scot **John Boyd Dunlop**: *1840-1921*.

The speedometer: invented by **Sir Keith Elphinstone**. *1864-1944*.

The modern road surface: **John McAdam**. *1756-1836*.

The steam car: **William Murdoch**. *1754-1839*.

The road steamer: **Robert Thomson**. *1822-73*.

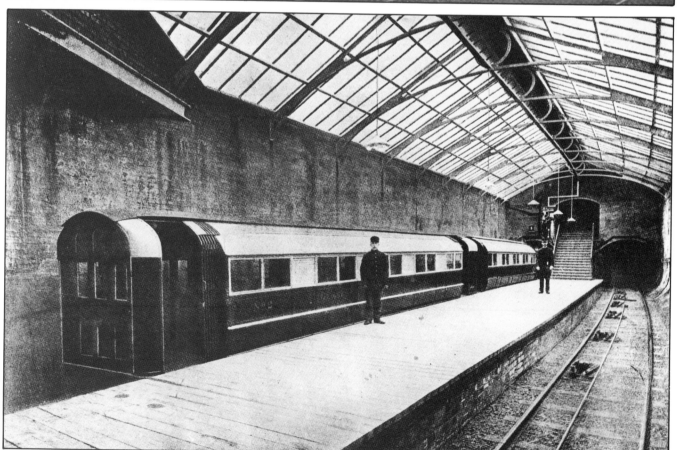

The first cable underground was in Glasgow.
ack: Museum of Transport, Glasgow.

Making the World Smaller

JOHN LOGIE BAIRD

*"I hate television. I hate it as much as
I hate eating peanuts.
But I still eat peanuts."*
Orson Welles

Making the World Smaller

Orson Welles may have had a love/hate relationship with television but it is thanks to two Scots, John Logie Baird and Archibald Campbell Swinton, that Citizen Kane is truly a citizen of the world.

The Scots both at home and abroad have played a major part in making the world smaller by improving the speed of communication through the centuries. Some of the most modern means of communication such as the video recorder and facsimile transmission have their roots in the Scots inventive mind. Somewhat surprising perhaps for a nation which has the reputation of being of few words.

The Scottish contribution to communications goes back to the 17th century with the oldest surviving envelope in the UK being sent from one Scot to another. In the 18th century, the great era of letter writing as a means of communication, Joseph Black significantly reduced the cost of writing paper, which had previously been made of linen, by introducing the means of manufacturing it by the chemical bleaching of rags. Perhaps it was on this type of notepaper, that another and anonymous Scot, known to the world simply as CM, wrote to the Scots Magazine in 1753 proposing the transmission of messages over a distance by means of a set of wires, each of which corresponded to a letter of the alphabet. No-one yet has been able to put a name to the man who so accurately forecast telegraphy.

James Watt is known throughout the world for his perfection of the steam engine. He is perhaps less widely known now for his invention of what became a standard piece of office equipment in the 19th century and which was in its way the forerunner of the photocopier.

The Letter Copier

James Watt *(1736-1819)* invented what is arguably the first duplicating machine in order to cope with the paperwork engendered by his growing engineering business. He first described his invention in a letter to his fellow Scot, Joseph Black.

"I have lately discovered a method of copying writing instantaneously, providing it has been written the same day or within twenty four hours. It enables me to copy all my business letters."

The device consisted of a flat bed press with either a side-arm lever or screw and a horizontal bar. The item to be copied was placed in the press with a piece of transparent tracing paper or unsized drawing paper, which had first been treated with a fixative of vinegar, borax, oystershells, bruised Aleppo galls and distilled water. The formula for this astringent was included in the patent that Watt took out on his invention in 1780. As the ink penetrated right through the unsized copying paper, the reverse impression of the text on the topside could be employed as a master for reproducing a number of duplicates on normal, sized paper. Thus Watt's copier can also be regarded as the first offset printing press.

The firm of James Watt and Company was formed in 1780 to take commercial advantage of the invention. Watt's partner, Matthew Boulton initiated an aggressive marketing campaign prior to the launch of the product. Promotional literature was circulated to all MPs and demonstrations of the copier were arranged at Westminster and at Court. Specimens of every kind of writing along with their duplicates were displayed at all the principal coffee houses. Not surprisingly, an unenthusiastic response was met with from the Governors of the Bank of England who were concerned at the risks of forgery. Boulton reacted with the comment, *"Some of their Directors are Hogs"*. A special, portable model was produced for travellers and a model designed for the Indian market with springs of best steel to withstand climatic changes.

In the first year of production, 150 models were sold, 20% for overseas. A special ink, mixed with mucilage was developed for supply in powdered form. Within a few years, the copier had become a standard piece of business equipment and machines varying very little from Watt's original prototype, continued in use in offices right up to the beginning of the 20th century. It was only the advent of carbon paper, stencils and xerography that spelt the end of the Watt copier.

As Watt is the father of the photocopier, another prolific Scots inventor, Alexander Bain is regarded as the father of facsimile transmission.

Alexander Bain *(1810-1877)*

A twin and a member of a Caithness crofting family of thirteen, Alexander Bain was apprenticed to a watchmaker in Wick where he acquired an interest in time that was to be with him all his life.

In 1837, he travelled to the other end of the country, to London, to finish his apprenticeship. In the evenings, he improved his scientific education by attending classes at the Polytechnic where his interests developed in the application of electricity to time transmission. His experiments sufficiently impressed the editor of the "Mechanics" magazine that he put Bain in touch with Charles Wheatstone, soon to win universal acclaim as the inventor of the telegraph. Their relationship started off cordially enough with Wheatstone paying Bain £3 for a model of Bain's telegraph and the promise of a further £50 on completion of the design. A lengthy quarrel, however, soon ensued when Wheatstone patented

Alexander Bain *(1810-1877).*
ack: Science Museum, London.

his own telegraph and opposed all Bain's attempts at patents, even for items in which he had no personal interest, such as Bain's mariners' log.

One patent that Bain successfully applied for, although even it was delayed, this time by one of Queen Victoria's confinements, was for the electric clock. He had developed a weight driven clock to make and break contacts and by use of a battery to send these impulses to drive various clock mechanisms connected by wires. He envisaged the universal distribution of Greenwich mean time by electricity. His electric clock and his subsequent invention in 1843 of the electro-magnetic pendulum did in fact lead to Greenwich mean time being adopted throughout the country. Previously each region had its own local time which may have been adequate in the more leisurely days of coach travel but was proving a drawback with the advent of the railways.

In 1844, he moved back to Scotland, setting up his workshop in the centre of Edinburgh. He set up a telegraph system for the Glasgow-Edinburgh railway and in 1846 demonstrated time transmission over this line. A pendulum in Edinburgh was utilised to work clocks in Glasgow.

At the same time as he patented his electro-magnetic pendulum, Bain also patented an automatic, chemical recording telegraph which recorded 282 words in fifty-two seconds at a subsequent demonstration between Lille and Paris. Further inventions in telegraphy included a telegraph that printed in plain type, a device that has in recent years earned Bain considerable credit as the first person to devise facsimile transmission. He also simplified the needle telegraph from five lines to one and devised a code for it: he was later to challenge Morse's patents for his code in the United States.

The historic quarrel with Wheatstone came to a head in 1847 when Wheatstone and his business partner Cooke promoted the Electric Telegraph Company and sought Parliamentary sanction for wayleave. Bain rose to the challenge—the most likely explanation is that they were both working independently towards the same solution—and the arguments were heard in both Houses of Parliament and the Courts of England, Scotland and Ireland before Wheatstone finally won the day. As some compensation to Bain, the Electric Telegraph Company was instructed to make and promote Bain's clock and give him half the profits.

Bain's last years were sad and disillusioned, although various attempts were made to provide him with a pension from the Civil List in acknowledgement of his contribution both to telegraphy and to time transmission.

The major preoccupation of Bain's life was with the telegraph. A year before his death a fellow Scot working in the United States patented an instrument which was in time to render the telegraph largely superfluous as a means of communication. The instrument was the telephone.

Alexander Graham Bell *(1847-1922)*

Interest in speech ran in the blood of the Bell family. Alexander Graham Bell's father and grandfather both studied the mechanics of speech and his father was a pioneer in the teaching of speech to the deaf. Alexander as a young man joined his father in his work at the Edinburgh School for the Deaf until tragedy struck the family in the shape of tuberculosis. Although Alexander, unlike two of his brothers, survived his health was poor and consequently in 1870 the family emigrated to Canada in an attempt to improve it.

From Canada, Bell crossed to the United States where in 1873 he was appointed Professor of Vocal Physiology at Boston University. Falling in love with one of his deaf pupils drove Bell's studies even harder, especially towards ways in which to reproduce sound mechanically. He hypothesised that if sound waves could be converted into a fluctuating electric current, that current could then be reconverted into sound waves identical with the original at the other end of the circuit. In this way sound could be carried across wires at the speed of light.

One day, while experimenting with a device that he had developed to test his theory, Bell accidentally spilled battery acid on his trousers. Without thinking, he called out to his assistant, *"Watson, please come here. I want you"*. Watson working at the other end of the circuit on another floor, heard the command and so was born the telephone.

In 1876, Bell patented his invention. It first went on public display at the Centennial Exhibition in Philadelphia where it became a major talking point. The first visitor of note to try it was the Brazilian Emperor, Pedro II, who instituted the first royal telephone conversation with the perhaps not immortal words *"By God, it talks"*. The next visitor was Lord Kelvin who was so impressed that he introduced the telephone to Britain. In no time, the telephone became part of the American scene and by the age of thirty Bell was rich and famous.

Bell did not rest on his laurels but continued to show an inventive streak of mind. He worked, for example, with Edison on the phonograph. In 1881, his inventive powers were summoned to a dramatic task. He devised a metal detecting device to locate the bullet in the body of President Garfield who was dying from the results of an assassination attempt. Although workable, the device failed on that occasion as no one thought to remove the steel springed mattress on which the President was lying.

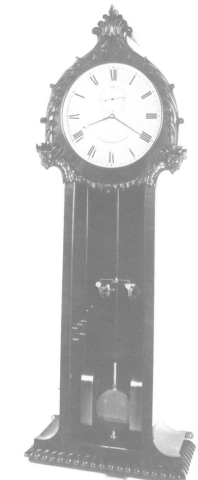

Alexander Bain's electric clock.
ack: Science Museum, London.

Alexander Graham Bell *(1847-1922).*
ack: The Telecom Technology Showcase, London.

Model of Alexander Graham Bell's original telephone 1875—patented in 1876.
ack: The Telecom Technology Showcase, London.

Making the World Smaller

First UK Telephone Exchange—Glasgow Medical Telephone Exchange 1879.

ack: Department of Medical Illustration, Glasgow Royal Infirmary.

Frederick George Creed (1871-1957).
ack: Glasgow Herald and Evening Times.

Bell's other interests included the founding of the American journal "Science," aeronautics and animal breeding. In 1915 when the first transcontinental telephone line was inaugurated, Bell repeated again the command to his assistant *"Watson, please come here. I want you"*. This time Watson was located at the other side of America.

The Scots were among the first to recognise the potential of Bell's telephone. This was due largely to the imagination of Lord Kelvin who although he had consumed much inventive energy in linking the two sides of the Atlantic by telegraph, recognised that the future lay with this even more effective form of communication.

The Telephone Exchange

The first telephone exchange in the UK was the Glasgow Medical Telephone Exchange established by the Glasgow firm of electrical engineers, Messrs. D and G Graham in January or February 1879. The first London exchange, which was the first in the UK to open to general subscribers, was not established until August of that year.

Messrs. D and G Graham pioneered the introduction of both telephony and the electric light to Scotland. The first telephone exchange was established at 140 Douglas Street—later immortalised in the "Douglas" central Glasgow telephone numbers—early in 1879 under the name of the Glasgow Medical Telephone Exchange. At first, the service was to be used exclusively by doctors, chemists and others such as hospitals, involved in the medical field. Night and Sunday services were available from the outset, affording the opportunity to call up a doctor at any time of night or day.

To this were quickly added "Legal", "Stockbrokers" and "Commercial" exchanges for members of the respective business groups. Independent switching facilities were initially provided for each of these groups but ultimately inter-communication links were set up. Subscribers had to agree to sign a five year contract with the exchange to protect Graham's interests against possible competition. Supplies of instruments were first obtained from the Bell Telephone Syndicate but when they themselves set up a rival exchange in Glasgow they declined to continue to supply Messrs Graham who then adopted the Gower Bell loud speaking telephone.

The necessary lines of single wire with earth return ran overhead. Wrought iron tubular poles were soon introduced to support the necessary wires. Graham further protected himself against competition by guaranteeing to keep in a reasonable state of repair the roofs of all the buildings that he made use of provided that no competitor was allowed access to them.

Graham's were also connected with the early development of the electric light in Scotland. They retained Lord Kelvin as consulting electrician and they were responsible for wiring Lord Kelvin's home for electricity, the first house in Scotland to be wired for the purpose. They were also responsible for generating the electricity for Swan's demonstration of the electric light to the meeting of the Philosophical Society of Glasgow in 1881.

The first mine in the world to be illuminated by electric light was fitted out by the company in 1881—the Earnock Colliery near Hamilton. At the same time they installed telephonic communication in the mine between the engine room and the pit face.

Bell took his inventive Scottish streak with him when he emigrated to the United States. The same streak travelled further with Frederick Creed, the inventor of the teleprinter.

Frederick George Creed (1871-1957)

Frederick Creed was the next best thing to Scottish. He was born in Nova Scotia, a predominantly Scottish settlement, to humble parents who had emigrated to Canada from Scotland. He left school at fourteen to qualify as a telegraph operator, working in Canada, Chile and Peru where he met his wife, Jeannie Russell who was working there as a Free Church of Scotland missionary.

At the time Morse code signals were transmitted from punched paper tape which involved the use of a Morse "stick" perforator, a device with three keys which were hit by hand held punches. In common with many other operators, Creed suffered from a permanently distorted right hand as a result of his occupation and it was this that made him start to think in the inventive mould.

He returned to Scotland in 1897. Here, having sought employment with the Glasgow Herald as a telegraph operator, Creed tried to interest influential people with his idea for a Morse based, telegraphic keyboard perforator. Kelvin surprisingly perhaps was unconvinced and Creed next tried the assistant editor of the Glasgow Herald with similar lack of success. Undaunted, Creed bought an old Burlick typewriter for fifteen shillings and spent much of his spare time over the next year converting it into a pneumatically powered keyboard perforator. This time Kelvin was impressed and offered him technical assistance to develop his idea further.

By this time, Creed had given up his job with the Herald and rented a workshop for the princely rent of five shillings, advertising his business with the slogan "Creed—makers of telegraphic equipment". An early success was the sale of twelve keyboard perforators to the General Post Office. He also soon convinced his ex-employers of the practicality of his invention. In addition to buying his equipment, the Herald gave him the freedom of their office to test his latest invention, a receiver perforator which received incoming signals on a perforated tape identical to that used at the other end for the transmission, and a printer that accepted the received message tape and decoded it into plain language characters on ordinary paper tape.

As business increased, Creed took the well trodden path south. In 1909, he opened a small factory in Croydon in the outskirts of London where he would be closer to the major potential markets for his invention, notably the Post Office. The company went from strength to strength, the newspaper industry being the first to seize on this new form of rapid communication, the teleprinter. In the ensuing years Creed further developed on his invention with Europe's first, start-stop, five unit code teleprinter, the automatic tape transmitter and the send/receive teleprinter.

Creed's latter years were offset by disappointment. In 1927 his successful firm was bought out by ITT and Creed soon fell out with his American directors. Among other reasons, Creed a strict Sabbatarian, disapproved strongly of the introduction of Sunday sports for employees. He resigned and turned his mind to inventions such as various types of catamaran and a twin-hulled seadrome for refuelling aircraft on Transatlantic flights: none was accepted in the commercial world. His last years were spent using all his resources to fight off impending bankruptcy.

The teleprinter helped the journalist to get the world's news to the breakfast table. Now, with television, the news can reach its audience at any time of day.

John Logie Baird (1888-1946)

Born in Helensburgh, it was from his attic workshop in Frith Street in London that Baird made the first television transmission of a moving image with gradations of light and shade, on 30 October 1925.

He had previously succeeded in transmitting the shadow of a Maltese Cross over a distance of ten feet in 1924, in his laboratory in Hastings. He was later evicted after an explosion caused by his electric supply which consisted of several hundred torch batteries wired together to form a 2000V power source. His original apparatus was made up of a tea chest, an empty biscuit box, Nipkow scanning discs made from cardboard, darning needles, hat boxes, cycle lamp lenses, discarded electric motors, piano wire, glue, string and sealing wax, all to a total value of about two shillings and sixpence.

While experimenting with a dummy's head on the night of 30 October, Baird received an image on the screen: *"Not as a mere smudge of black and white but as a real image with detail."* In his excitement he rushed down to the office below in quest of a live model. He came back with an office boy, William Taynton. Baird

John Logie Baird (1888-1946).
First television transmissions of moving image 1925.
ack: National Galleries of Scotland, Edinburgh.

Baird Televisor *c.* 1926.
ack: Museum of Transport, Glasgow.

described what happened next in an interview that he gave in the USA six years later:

"I placed him before the transmitter and went into the next room to see what the screen would show. The screen was entirely blank and no effort of tuning would produce any results. Puzzled and disappointed I went back to the transmitter and there the cause of the failure became at once evident. The boy, scared by the intense white light had backed away from the transmitter. In the excitement of the moment I gave him half a crown and this time he kept his head in the right position. Going again into the next room this time I saw his head quite clearly. It is curious that the first person in the world to have been seen by television should have required a bribe to accept that distinction."

Baird gave his first demonstration of true television to the Press in January 1926 and on the next day he gave his first public demonstration before some forty members of the Royal Institution. Dr Alexander Russell of Faraday House wrote up Baird's achievement in the issue of "Nature" of 3 July 1926.

"We saw the transmission by television of living human faces, the proper gradation of light and shade and all movements of the head, of the lips and mouth and of a cigarette and its smoke were faithfully portrayed on a screen in the theatre, the transmitter being in a room at the top of the building. Naturally, the results are far from perfect. The image cannot be compared with that of a good kinematograph film. The likeness, however, was unmistakable and all the motions are reproduced with absolute fidelity. This is the first time that we have seen real television and . . . . Mr Baird is the first to have accomplished this marvellous feat."

Baird's system of television employed a mechanical scanner in both the transmitting apparatus and the receiver. Although Baird eventually lost the race to produce a viable system of high resolution television, he had undoubtedly shown others the way. Whether or not he is accepted as the inventor of television his claim to priority in achieving the dream of "seeing by wireless" is indisputable.

Baird also made the first television transmission in colour, from the Baird studios on 3 July 1928. The pictures he showed included scarves, a policeman's helmet, a man putting his tongue out, the glowing end of a cigarette and a bunch of red roses. His low definition system employed a Nipkow scanning disc with red, blue and green filters. In later life, he even experimented with the possibility of 3-D colour television.

Another example of how Baird's ideas raced ahead of the market was Phonovision, developed by him in 1928. This, the first television recording system, allowed for low frequency signals to be reproduced on aluminium discs using either two separate discs for sound and vision or a single, double tracked disc. The idea was to record programmes which could be purchased by the public and played back by means of a simple attachment to their Baird Televisor sets. Baird anticipated the development of video cassettes but although the principle of his system was sound, it was too early to be commercially practicable. By 1935 television recordings on disc were being advertised for sale giving six minutes of recording on each side: a disc cost seven shillings. As Baird had been too precipitate, the initiator of this enterprise, one R O Hughes, proved to be too late. Four months after he had launched his recordings on the market, Baird's low definition television transmissions were discontinued and the majority of viewers, many of whom had constructed their own sets from kits, proceeded to dismantle them.

Baird did not in fact invent the television of today. His television was based on a mechanical system which has since been superceded by the more effective electronic system. It was, however, fellow Scot, **Archibald Campbell Swinton,** who laid down the principles of modern television. As early as 1908 he proposed the use of cathode ray tubes, magnetically reflected at both camera and receiver, to transmit and receive images.

Robert Watson-Watt's contribution to communications was of a very different nature. He took the developing science of electronics and applied it to create radar.

Sir Robert Watson-Watt (1892-1973)

Born in the Angus town of Brechin, Watson-Watt first studied and then lectured at his local university of St Andrews.

From his earliest days he showed an interest in the reflection of radio waves. Based on the knowledge that their reflection was sharper as wavelengths decreased, Watson-Watt took out a patent as early as 1919 in connection with radio location by means of short-wave radio. Throughout the 1920's he worked on improvements to his patent and by 1935 had produced a system that made it possible to follow an aircraft by the radio-wave reflection that it sent back. He christened the system "radio detection and ranging", soon to be shortened to "radar".

With the war clouds beginning to form over Europe, the military significance of radar was soon grasped and Watson-Watt's research went underground. Successful trials of the new system were carried out on a remote airfield on the

Alan Archibald Campbell Swinton laid down the principles of modern television.
ack: National Portrait Gallery, London.

Sir Robert Watson-Watt (1892-1973).
ack: The Trustees of the Imperial War Museum, London.

Suffolk coast. As part of the cloak of secrecy surrounding the project, it was put about that it was simply a piece of ionospheric research and was given the public description of Radio Direction Finding. Ironically, this deceit became truth: it had not at first been realised that the direction of an aircraft as well as its distance could be determined by the new device.

Radar came into its own in the Second World War. It made it possible during the Battle of Britain to detect enemy planes in all weathers and as easily by night as by day. Although the United States and Germany had also been developing radar type systems, it was Watson-Watt's research and the pressures of war that gave Britain the lead. In 1941, Watson-Watt visited the United States and helped them to complete their radar systems. Radar gave warning of the onset of enemy planes at Pearl Harbour in 1941 but the warning was tragically ignored.

Radar has since developed many peacetime uses from aircraft navigation and security systems to the detection of stormy weather.

With all the sophistication of modern telecommunications, the postage stamp still has its humble part to play. The simple act of sticking a stamp on a letter is due to an Arbroath born bookseller.

James Chalmers (1782-1853)

The world's first adhesive postage stamp was printed by James Chalmers at his Dundee printing works in 1834 as a sample to illustrate his idea for standardising the prepayment of postage. Initially he failed to arouse any interest. He submitted several examples of the stamp to the Parliamentary Select Committee set up to consider Rowland Hill's proposals for the reform of the postal service. Hill's original suggestion for prepayment had been envelopes with stamps printed on them. Surviving proofs show Chalmers' stamp to have been a sepia coloured square bearing the legend—"General Postage—NOT EXCEEDING HALF AN OUNCE—One Penny" enclosed in a decorative border. Chalmers used one of his sample twopenny stamps on a letter posted to the Secretary of the GPO. This was the first time that an envelope bearing an adhesive stamp ever went through the mails.

To this day, there has been controversy as to whether Chalmers or Rowland Hill actually invented the adhesive postage stamp. It would seem that Chalmers was the first actually to produce a sample in 1834 and Rowland Hill to suggest the idea in print in 1837. Whoever wins, the General Post Office introduced adhesive stamps for general use in 1840 with its issue of the Penny Black and Twopenny Blue.

Radar aerial.
ack: The Trustees of the Imperial War Museum, London.

James Chalmers (1782-1853).
The first adhesive postage stamp printed at his works in Dundee, 1834.
ack: City of Dundee District Council, Art Galleries and Museums Department..

Chalmers' printing press.
ack: City of Dundee District Council, Art Galleries and Museums Department..

Communications

The modern light condensing system in lighthouses: **Alan Stevenson.** *1807-65.*
Radar: **Sir Robert Watson-Watt.** *1892-1973.*
The letter copier: **James Watt.** *1736-1819.*
The first telephone exchange in the UK: Glasgow Medical Telephone Exchange. *1879.*
The first motor mail van service: Argyllshire. *1896.*
The first post office in the UK: operating since 1783 at Sanquhar.
Broadcasting: **Sir John Reith.**
Facsimile transmission: **Alexander Bain.** *1810-77.*
First demonstration of television: **John Logie Baird.** *1888-1946.*
Proposal of the electric telegraph: **CM.** *1753.*
Proposal of wireless telegraphy: **James Bowman Lindsay.** *1845.*
First international TV transmission: **John Logie Baird.** *1888-1946.*
The adhesive postage stamp: **James Chalmers.** *1782-1853.*
The automatic chemical telegraph. **Alexander Bain.** *1810-77.*
Colour television. **John Logie Baird.** *1888-1946.*
First television recording system. **John Logie Baird.** *1888-1946.*
The postmark: **James Chalmers.** *1782-1853.*
The teleprinter: **Frederick Creed.** *1871-1957.*
Video recording: **John Logie Baird.** *1888-1946.*
The modern system of television: **Archibald Campbell Swinton.** *1863-1930.*

First post office in Britain, operating since 1763 at Sanquhar, Dumfriesshire.
ack: Sanquhar Museum.

Inventor of

J. Chalmers.

THE ADHESIVE STAMP

Example of the adhesive stamp.
James Chalmers.
ack: City of Dundee District Council, Art Galleries and Museums Department..

James Watt—first copying press (duplicating machine).
ack: Trustees of the Science Museum, London.

Fuelling the
Industrial Revolution

JAMES YOUNG

"At the beginning of our works we had great difficulty in getting people to use this oil."
James Young

Fuelling the Industrial Revolution

David Dale (1739-1806).
ack: National Galleries of Scotland, Edinburgh.

Robert Owen (1771-1858).
ack: New Lanark Conservation Trust.

One wonders what James Young would have thought today of the headlines about energy crises, political tensions in the Middle East and the oil economy. How would he have reacted to the mammoth structures of the North Sea pumping oil from the fields named after Scottish geologists like Hutton and Murchison. One suspects that with his sound head for business, he would have thoroughly approved.

Scotland has always enjoyed an abundance of energy resources. The wood from its forests fuelled the early iron furnaces: the water from its rivers drove the early machinery. It was its closeness to the River Clyde that caused David Dale to select New Lanark as the site for the cotton mills that under the management of his son-in-law, Robert Owen, were to become the cradle of industrial welfare. Water too powered the Industrial Revolution ushered in by James Watt. It was Watt's assistant, William Murdoch, who laid the commercial foundations of the gas industry.

William Murdoch (1754-1839)

Son of a millwright in Auchinleck in Ayrshire, Murdoch went south in 1777 to join the firm of Boulton and Watt. He was attracted by the growing reputation of Watt's steam engines which were beginning to enjoy commercial success. His enthusiasm outmatched his meagre finances. When he sought an interview with Watt to take him on as an apprentice, he put his hat on the table with a thud. When Watt commented on the noise it made, Murdoch replied "I turned it myself". He was determined to look the part even if it meant having to construct his hat out of a piece of wood. Murdoch was dispatched to Cornwall to supervise the installation of the engines in the local tin mines. He prospered and by 1800 had become a partner in the concern.

While working with Boulton and Watt, Murdoch suggested many successful improvements to the steam engine including the sun and planet wheel, the bell crank engine and the slide valve, which improved the compactness of the steam engine. While based in Birmingham, he joined a group of scientists including Watt, Joseph Priestley and Erasmus Darwin who met regularly to discuss scientific and philosophical topics. The group was liberal in outlook. Its meetings came to a sudden end when Priestley's house was burned down by a mob in 1791.

Murdoch's most lasting contribution lay in another direction. He was the first person to see in coal something more than a simple solid fuel. In 1792 he began to experiment with heating coal, peat and wood in the absence of air and to store the gases that were given off. By 1800 Murdoch had set up an experimental gas light using coal gas: he was the first person to light his house by gas. In 1802, he celebrated the temporary peace treaty signed with Napoleon by organising a spectacular display of gas lighting and by 1805 he was routinely lighting his main

Robert Owen's school for children, 1819.
ack: New Lanark Conservation Trust.

New Lanark's Counting House seen during the annual Victorian Fair.
ack: New Lanark Conservation Trust.

Right: New Lanark. c. 1900.
ack: New Lanark Conservation Trust.

factory by gas. Its potential was quickly realised and as early as 1807 some London streets were lit by gas.

Murdoch is a classic example of the "Jack of all trades" who was in fact master of several: another is **James Neilson**. Although Neilson's main contribution to the industrial growth of his country was the hot blast, he also gave the early Victorians the means to light their houses with his fishtail gas burner. Although Murdoch is the true founder of the modern gas industry, another Scot of a very different kind was one of the first to manufacture gas. Although he realised its commercial value, the nature of his inventive and restless personality did not allow him to follow up his discovery.

Archibald Cochrane, 9th Earl of Dundonald *(1749-1831)*

Although he was a Fife aristocrat and Admiral in the British navy, Cochrane's real abilities lay as an industrial chemist. He laid down the foundations of many processes that were to provide the chemicals demanded by 19th century industrial production. Owing to a combination of bad luck and a certain lack of basic business sense, Cochrane saw few of his ideas bear fruit in his lifetime.

It was in 1781 that he first patented the distillation of tar from coal. This process which he carried out in a small tar distillery in Culross, a village on the Forth estuary which for centuries had local coal mining and salt panning industries, yielded many products of crucial importance in the coming century. They included tar, varnish, lamp black, coke and gas. Dundonald was undoubtedly aware of the illuminating properties of the gas but with his naval background was more interested in persuading the Admiralty to use the tar as a wood preservative for ship's bottoms. His words went unheeded.

He had no greater success in persuading the Admiralty to adopt another of his many ideas, the smokescreen. The Admiralty rejected it on the grounds that it would be an ungentlemanly way of conducting naval warfare. Dundonald's formula lay dormant in their files for a century until it was unearthed and put into operation in the middle of the 1914-18 war. Another of his ideas was also initially unsuccessful—the process for manufacturing caustic soda from soap makers' leys. Alkali soda, one of the basic chemicals of 19th century manufacturing processes, had previously been extracted from seaweed at great cost and in very small quantities. Dundonald's process allowed for its production much more cheaply and efficiently from common salt but like so many of his ideas it was left for others to take up.

His son, who inherited not only his father's title, but his passion for the sea and his innovative mind, is today best known as the founder of several South American navies. He too, however, played a part in the history of energy production. He became involved with the American geologist, Dr Abraham Gesner, in a project to produce gas and related by-products from the Great Pitch Lake of Trinidad. He named the resulting clarified pitch, kerosene, derived from the Greek word for wax. Gesner later re-used the word to describe paraffin.

Another Scot, cast somewhat in the Cochrane mould, may have an even stronger claim to a place of honour in the history of energy—a little known Dundee polymath who appears to have produced continuous electric light 35 years before Swan and Edison.

James Bowman Lindsay *(1799-1862)*

Both Joseph Swan and Thomas Edison have their supporters in the fight for the title of "Father of the Electric Light". The prize may in fact belong to a little known inventor from Dundee who claims to have produced continuous electric light as early as 1835.

There seems little doubt that James Bowman Lindsay who remains a rather elusive and eccentric figure in the history of invention did achieve some form of electric lighting which he demonstrated to the public in a series of evening lectures at the Thistle Hall in Dundee. The reporter, sent along by the local paper to cover the event, wrote enthusiastically the next day:

"Mr Lindsay, a teacher in town, succeeded on the evening of Saturday, July 25 in obtaining a constant electric light.... The light in beauty surpasses all others, has no smell, emits no smoke, is incapable of explosion and, not requiring air for combustion, can be kept in sealed glass jars.... It can be sent to any convenient distance and the apparatus for producing it can be contained in a common chest."

Lindsay himself in a letter to the newspaper shed a little more light on his invention. *"I am writing this letter by means of it at six inches or eight inches distant; and at the present moment can read a book at the distance of one and a half feet. From the same apparatus I can get two or three lights, each of which is fit for reading with. I can make it burn in the open air or in a glass tube without air and neither wind nor water is capable of extinguishing it."*

Unfortunately, little more is known of Lindsay's invention and none of his scientific apparatus has survived. Scientists have puzzled for many years as to what he actually discovered. Was it simply an unusual form of arc lighting or was it the true forerunner of the electric light? Lindsay himself had the vision to

William Murdoch *(1754-1839)*.
ack: National Galleries of Scotland, Edinburgh.

William Murdoch laid the commercial foundations of the gas industry.

Top: Murdoch's first factory gasworks, 1806.
Below: Murdoch lights his home.
ack: Trustees of the Science Museum, London.

Fuelling the Industrial Revolution

foretell the day when *"its beauty will recommend itself to the fashionable: and the producing apparatus, framed, may stand side by side with the piano in the drawing room.... and being capable of surpassing all lights in its splendour it will be used in lighthouses and for telegraphs"*. Having achieved his ambition of creating continuous electric light, Lindsay directed his attention to one of his many other projects, the production of a Pentecontaglossal Dictionary. His publication of the Lord's Prayer in fifty languages may be seen more as a monument to his tireless perseverence than as a contribution to practical philology.

Lindsay's whole life is divided between diligent pursuit of pointless goals such as his mammoth "Chrono-Astrolabe", a full set of astronomical tables intended to assist in the calculation of chronological periods, and flashes of genius. For a time he became interested in wireless telegraphy and succeeded in transmitting messages across the Tay at a distance of some miles. Although his methods were not likely to bear fruit his vision did succeed in achieving for him an acknowledgement from Marconi and a small place in the history of telegraphy as the first man to propose linking Britain and America through the medium of wireless telegraphy.

Steam power, gas, electricity.... and oil, the fuel of the 20th century, first refined by a Scottish chemist, who unlike Cochrane and Lindsay was fully aware of the commercial potential of his discovery and exploited it to the full.

James "Paraffin" Young (1811-1883)

James Young was born and brought up in Glasgow. While Young was training as a young man to be a joiner and instrument maker, his scientific curiosity took him to classes at Glasgow University held by Thomas Graham, probably the most noted chemical theorist of his day. When Graham moved to London, Young followed him as his assistant. He then turned his own theoretical knowledge to practical use by working for two major chemical manufacturers, thereby picking up an expertise in industrial processes that was to stand him in very good stead.

In 1847, a mutual friend, Professor Lyon Playfair, put Young in touch with his brother-in-law who had discovered a natural oil spring in one of his Derbyshire mines. Young experimented with the distillation of the oil and prepared paraffin wax, naphtha, light oil and lubricating oil from the seepage. Playfair persuaded Young to make him a couple of candles from the paraffin and set them one at each side of him when delivering a paper to the Royal Institution. Young kept the remains of one of the candles as a memento of the origin of what was to become one of the largest chemical industries in modern times.

Realising that the source of oil would soon be exhausted, Young turned his mind to the distillation potential of other materials and found that cannel coal was the most suited to his purpose. In this experiment he postulated the chemical law relating to the destructive distillation of coal. In 1850 he formed a partnership to set up a processing plant near Bathgate which was sited over a rich seam of cannel coal. Thus the world's first oil refinery was created. Production of oil and paraffin started in time for samples to be displayed at the Great Exhibition of 1851. In 1850 Young took out patents for the heating and subsequent distillation and processing of bituminous coal to form paraffin. Thus, he anticipated the drilling of the first oil well in the US by nine years.

He surrounded his operations with strict security, a necessary precaution as his patents were being constantly challenged, due to the fact that his process yielded profits as high as ninety two per cent over costs. The emergent oil industry in the US frequently had to call on Young for the licence to process kerosene to his techniques which had proved to be the most efficient. Young was on several occasions offered partnerships by US oil companies which he steadfastly rejected thus depriving himself of the opportunity to beat Rockefeller to the title of "oil tycoon". He was content to rest in the knowledge that one day he would earn the title of *"Father of the Oil Industry"*.

Ironically, it was partly the increasing cost of cannel coal, which was being forced up by the import demands of the US processors of kerosene by Young's methods, that forced Young to look for another source of oil. This he found in shale. Although shale gave a much lower yield than cannel coal, it was available in West Lothian in almost unlimited quantities. By 1864, when his original patents ran out, Young's shale oil plant was in full swing. Thereafter occurred what has been described as the *"Scottish oil mania"*: by 1870, ninety seven oil companies were operating in West Lothian. Young himself gradually retired from the business, devoting his leisure to his many other interests which included a proposal for a Channel tunnel, research into light waves and financial support for the African ventures of his friend, David Livingstone.

Murdoch and Young's legacy lives on today in Scotland in the multi-million North Sea oil and gas fields, in the petrochemical industry around the shores of the Firth of Forth and in the experimental coal gasification plant in Fife. Their legacy has ensured Scotland's position as an exporter of energy until well into the 21st century.

James "Paraffin" Young *(1811-1883)*.
Father of the oil industry.
ack: Strathclyde University Archives, Glasgow.

Of Things Domestic

THE MACINTOSH

"A sort of smock frock of India rubber cloth."
Charles Macintosh

Of Things Domestic

No, the Scots did not invent the dish washer, the deep freeze or the breakfast cereal. They did, however, invent the process for water softening, the principle of refrigeration and oatmeal porridge!

It may be haggis, bagpipes and the kilt that people associate with Scotland's contribution to daily life but Scots have been responsible for some rather more essential and functional items too. The most essential and functional feature of households worldwide indeed bears the trademark of an innovative Scottish sanitary engineer.

How would the busy housewife thicken her sauce without cornflour, first produced in Paisley in 1854? How would the Englishman swallow his toast without marmalade, or the American sightsee without his Mac? The American may have arrived on a cruise, and affixed a stamp to send his postcard back home; the cruise, the stamp and the postcard were all available courtesy of Messrs Anderson, Chalmers and MacDonald. He may sit down for a glass of what he thinks of as his national soft drink, but which turns out to be half-Scottish in inspiration. Or he may fancy something stronger, a whisky lengthened with some Canada Dry and for his wife a vodka and lime. Both mixers also came from Scotland. He leaves his finger prints on the glass; another Scot has ensured that he leaves his identity too.

The following paragraphs describe just a few of the Scottish contributions to daily life.

The Macintosh

The son of a Glasgow chemical manufacturer, **Charles Macintosh** *(1766-1843)* followed in his father's footsteps becoming Britain's largest producer of alum, the mordaunt used in dyeing.

Like several other manufacturers, Macintosh became interested in the waterproofing of fabrics. His factory was producing a waterproofed fabric, consisting of two layers of cloth glued together with a solution of india rubber dissolved in naphtha. It proved impossible, however, to tailor such an unwieldy sandwich. Coincidentally, James Syme, a medical student at Edinburgh University, who was to become an outstanding and innovative surgeon, discovered a more practical method of dissolving rubber using a by-product of coal tar. In 1823, Macintosh obtained the rights to patent the process and so gave birth to the garment that bears his name.

Important early commissions included the outfitting of Sir John Franklin's expedition to the Arctic in 1824 for which Macintosh made the world's first inflatable lifejacket and the first rubber airbed. Until 1830 when he amalgamated with the Manchester firm of Thomas Hancock, Macintosh confined himself to the production of the waterproof cloth for individual tailors to make up. From 1830 he and his partner moved into the ready-to-wear market.

In some ways they were unlucky. The macintosh offered the ideal protection against the elements necessary for stagecoach travel but this was to be shortly superceded by the comforts of the railway carriage. There were also numerous complaints about the ungainliness and peculiar smell emitted by the garments and their tendency to melt in hot weather. This last objection was finally overcome when Hancock patented the vulcanisation process for rubber in 1843. Over the following decades, other manufacturers resolved the problems of shape and smell satisfactorily. The name remains, often affectionately shortened, in honour of its Scots originator, the "Mac".

The Kaleidoscope

The kaleidoscope reflects the kaleidoscopic nature of its inventor's talents. **Sir David Brewster** *(1781-1868)* was not only an experimental scientist of international repute but also a writer, university administrator and founder of The British Association for the Advancement of Science.

He was born and brought up in Jedburgh, a small town in the Scottish Borders. His father, headmaster of the local Grammar school, must have been a formidable character; he insisted that all four of his sons trained for the ministry. While at University, Brewster's interest in science developed rapidly. In 1799 he wrote to a friend in Jedburgh *"I have finished the electrical machine but cannot make it give a shock"*. His interest in science coupled with his nervousness in the pulpit—he succumbed to faintness when preaching—led him to adopt a journalistic career as editor of the "Edinburgh Magazine" later to become the "Edinburgh Journal of Science".

His literary career did not preclude his pursuit of scientific interests which lay in the theory of light, optical instrumentation, and the relationship between colour and temperature. To the scientific world he is best known for the law of polarisation of bi-axial crystals that bears his name. He laid the foundations for the modern study of crystallography and experimental optics. His methodology was innovative and his empirical approach led him to devise his theories on the basis of repeated experiment.

He did not confine himself to the theoretical sphere. In 1808 he wrote *"I have lately been attending much to optics and have invented several new instruments"*. His practical inventions included several new types of

Riding macintosh, light blue with blue velvet collar and cuffs. "A sort of smock frock of Macintosh's India rubber cloth." 1839.

ack: English Costumes for Sports and Outdoor Recreation. Phillis Cunnington and Alan Mansfield. A. & C. Black Publishers Ltd.

micrometer, the dioptic lens which proved to be a major innovation in lighthouse illumination and the stereoscope which was on show at the Great Exhibition and became a popular craze, counting Queen Victoria among its adherents. It is, however, for the kaleidoscope that Brewster is most widely known. He patented it in 1814 hoping to make a great deal of money from the sale. Unfortunately, however, the patent was not watertight and soon every instrument maker was copying it. As he wrote to his wife, *"You can form no conception of the effect which the instrument excited in London. Infants are seen carrying them in their hands, the coachmen in their boxes are busy using them,....and thousands of poor people make their bread by selling them....Had I managed my patents rightly, I would have made £100,000 by it"*.

Brewster married the daughter of James MacPherson, the Scottish poet who claimed to have found the legendary poems of Ossian: he, in fact, wrote them himself. In 1831, Brewster was knighted for his scientific achievements but only after he received a royal assurance that the associated fee of £109 would be waived. In later life, he became Principal of St Andrews University, a post which at the time was regarded as a sinecure. Brewster, however, was too active a personality to accept this and he tried, not entirely successfully, to reform the University administration. In 1859, he became Principal of Edinburgh University at double the salary, a post which he retained until his death in 1868. The inscription on his tombstone was well chosen: the first verse of Psalm XXVII *"The Lord is my light"*.

Bovril

James Lawson Johnston was a Scot who emigrated to Canada. In 1874, at Sherbrooke in Quebec Province, he first manufactured on a commercial scale his "fluid beef". Ten years later he returned to Britain and started production of his meat extract in a factory in Trinity Square, London. Determined to lift his product from an obscure fluid beef extract to a household name, he picked the name "Bovril", a combination of the Latin "bo" or ox and Vrilya, the name given to the life force in a little known novel by Bulwer Lytton. The first advertisement for the new product read:

"ONE OUNCE of the nutritious constituents of JOHNSTON'S FLUID BEEF, brand BOVRIL, contains more real direct nourishment than FIFTY OUNCES of ordinary meat extract, and FIVE HUNDRED GUINEAS will be forfeited if this statement can be refuted."

From then on, the word Bovril was used on its own and was on its way to becoming a household name. In the 1890's it survived an attack by the Scottish chain store millionaire, Sir Thomas Lipton, who decided to manufacture his own version of the product undercutting Bovril's prices by thirty five per cent. By 1914, however, Bovril was back in Lipton's stores: he managed to negotiate a sufficiently large trade discount with the Bovril company to render continued production of his "own brand" uneconomic.

Bovril 1874.
James Lawson Johnston.
ack: Bovril Ltd.

Fingerprinting—a technique in criminal investigation first advocated by Henry Faulds.
ack: Strathclyde Police.

Fingerprinting

Born in Beith in Ayrshire, **Henry Faulds** *(1843-1930)* trained as a doctor and spent many years of his life in Japan.

It was while he was employed as a physician at the Tsukiji Hospital in Tokyo, that Faulds started to make a study of fingerprint techniques. In a letter to "Nature" published on the 28 October 1880 he wrote:

"When bloody finger marks or impressions on clay, glass etc. exist they may lead to the scientific investigation of criminals. Already I have had experience in two such cases and found useful evidence from these marks. In one case greasy finger marks revealed who had been drinking rectified spirit. The pattern was unique and fortunately I had previously obtained a copy of it. They agreed with microscopic fidelity. In another case sooty finger marks of a person climbing a white wall were of great use as negative evidence."

Fauld's letter immediately revealed that William Herschel, an Indian civil servant, had also been researching in this field. Faulds spent much of his life making vitriolic attacks on Herschel and his supporters as the sole pioneer of fingerprinting. Certainly Faulds was the first person to advocate the use of fingerprints in criminal investigation whereas Herschel saw the technique only as a device to detect impersonation. The prestigious role of "Nature" has led to the accepted belief among scientists that the person to publish in "Nature" has first claim to the innovation. Faulds failed in his attempt to interest the Police Commissioners in his discovery and the first police force to use fingerprinting was La Plata Division of the Provincial Police of Buenos Aires in 1891, using a different method of classification.

Faulds died in 1930 having turned down the post of personal physician to the Crown Prince of Japan. Little known in his native land, he is commemorated by a statue in Japan.

Kola Type Soft Drinks

There is some evidence to suggest that the Scots put the Cola into Coca Cola.

The first reference to kola type soft drinks is an article in the "Mineral Water Trade Review" of 1873 recommending manufacturers to use the seeds of the kola nut to form a syrup for lemonade. Although there is no conclusive evidence it is thought that it was the Scots who introduced the Kola flavour: certainly the drink was popular in Scotland by 1880. Scotland is probably the only place where Kola exists today as a soft drink and the drink is traditionally known in the trade as "Scotch Kola". In a privately owned formulae book there is a recipe of 1880 for "Edinburgh Kola" and several Scottish soft drinks companies who are still manufacturing Kola today were manufacturing such soft drinks around 1880.

In 1879, an American trade writer recorded that *"In Scotland they have a drink called Kola in which extracts from the nuts and leaves of the African cola tree are used. It is much thought of by the natives and is flavoured in various ways after the fashion of meads, sherberts and sherries. It could presumably be tried in the United States of America by any enterprising bottler".*

About this time, American soft drink manufacturers were beginning to produce coca flavoured drinks derived from the leaves of the Brazilian coca shrub. Indeed two American chemists carried on an acrimonious correspondence, each claiming that he was the originator of coca flavoured drinks in the late 1870's.

It was an Atlanta chemist, John Pemberton, who in trying to devise a new blend of soft drink to be sold through soda fountain outlets, hit upon the idea of combining the flavours of coca and cola in 1884-85. Thus began the manufacture of Coca Cola.

The Grand Piano

John Broadwood *(1732-1812)* was born and brought up in the rural hamlet of Oldhamstocks on the border of East Lothian and Berwickshire. He followed in his father's trade as carpenter and joiner. He left the village at the age of twenty nine to seek fame and fortune with a letter of introduction in his pocket from the local laird to the London firm of harpsichord makers Burkhard Shudi. Broadwood proved such an excellent apprentice that soon he gained not only the hand of Shudi's daughter but also a partnership in the firm, now to be called "Burkhard Shudi et Johannes Broadwood". In 1771 Shudi formally handed over the running of the business to his son-in-law.

In the late 1770's Broadwood and his assistant Robert Stodart were working on a new piano action which was to become known as the English Grand Action. In 1777 in the name of Stodart, the first patent for the grand piano was taken out. For some time Broadwood was content to leave the development of the grand piano in Stodart's capable hands while he concentrated on improvements and modifications to the square piano. He took out a patent for "piano and forte pedals", thus giving birth to the piano pedal and doing away with the awkward hand and knee levers of existing models.

Satisfied with the improvements to the square piano, Broadwood then turned his mind to developing the grand. In order to improve the quality of the tone of the notes he introduced a separate bass bridge, an adaptation that was soon adopted by all piano makers. He next extended the range of the piano, introducing the

The grand piano.
The first patented grand piano in Britain: 1777.
ack: Sotheby's, London.

first, six octave grand in 1794. By the mid 1790's such was the success of the piano that Broadwood gave up harpsichord manufacture altogether. In 1811, he handed over the business to his two sons. The company to this day has continued the innovative tradition of musical instrument making that John Broadwood had established.

The Lawnmower

Although the very first mechanical lawnmower was produced by Edwin Budding of Gloucestershire, the first effective lawnmower was designed by an Arbroath engineer, **Alexander Shanks.** In 1841 he was commissioned by a local landowner to design a mower for his two and a half acre lawn. Shanks came up with a machine which could be pulled by a small pony without leaving hoofmarks on the grass and reduced the time taken by his client to cut his lawn to two and a half hours. Shanks' design represented a major step forward as it could be pulled rather than pushed and did not churn up the ground that it was intended to smooth. In 1842, Shanks patented his design thus giving added poignancy to the expression "Shanks' pony"; it was not until 1939 that horse drawn machines ceased to be used. Throughout the 19th century, animals were fitted with specially designed boots to be worn on grass cutting duties.

Lawnmower 1841.
Alexander Shanks.
ack: Arbroath Museum, Angus.

Shanks continued his innovative approach to lawnmower design over the next century. In 1856, he introduced a model with one wheel in front and a drive roller, which supplied the power via gearing at the rear of the machine. In 1862, he produced a two person model and in 1892, he introduced rear roller springing to cut down the vibration caused by the uneven lawns of the time. As well as lawnmowers for domestic use, he produced a special range of heavy duty machines for parks and sports grounds: one of his most popular models, not surprisingly was the Golf Lynx for the fine cutting required by golf greens.

It cannot be said that the Scots let the grass grow under their feet! It was another Scot, **David Cockburn,** who designed the first successful rotary lawnmower, the forerunner of the mains powered, rotary mowers possessed by many households today.

Lawnmowers in front of Balmoral Castle.
ack: Arbroath Museum, Angus.

Lime Juice

For some reason, the history of lime juice and of Scotland have proved a fruitful mixture. It was the Edinburgh doctor, James Lind, who first recommended the use of lemon and lime juice as a specific against scurvy. It was fellow Scot, Sir Gilbert Blane, nicknamed "chillblain" by his colleagues for his somewhat reserved manner, who ensured that lime juice was a part of naval rations and who also invented a means of preserving lime juice on long voyages. It was **Lachlan Rose** who took the rum out of the lime ration and made lime juice the popular soft drink of today.

By trade, Rose was a member of a Leith family business in ship repair and chandlery supplies. In the same year as the Merchant Shipping Act made a ration of lime or lemon juice compulsory for all sailors, Rose took out a patent for his process of preserving fruit juices without the addition of alcohol. Until 1867, the juices were supplied to sailors unsweetened and laced with fifteen per cent of rum as a preserving agent.

Inspiration came to Rose from observing the fumigation of wine casks with burning sulphur: from this he devised a method for sulphiting juices and cordials. He realised also that by sweetening the cordials and packing them in attractive bottles, he could market his products to a wider public. And so, the first branded fruit juice was born.

Lime juice—preserving fruit juice without the addition of alcohol.
Lachlan Rose.
ack: Schweppes Ltd.

His company went from strength to strength. The range of fruit juices was quickly extended to include not only the already famous, Lime Juice Cordial, but more exotic drinks with names like Ginger Brandy, Rum Shrub and Orange Quinine Wine. In 1893 the company purchased its own estate on Dominica to guarantee a regular supply of limes and five years later, it became a limited company. In 1957, Rose's merged with Schweppes. Ironically, today, lime juice has returned to its alcoholic origins, being a popular mixer with vodka.

Marmalade

An essential part of the traditional British breakfast, marmalade was first produced in Dundee at the end of the 18th century.

Like many of the best known inventions, marmalade evolved from an error. **James Keiller** *(1775-1839),* a Dundee merchant purchased a consignment of bitter, Seville oranges from a ship that had put into port at Dundee. His wife, Janet, had reservations about the wisdom of his purchase and finally decided to make the oranges into a jelly similar to the way in which she treated quinces. The result was marmalade.

In 1797, James Keiller realising that his wife had created a winner out of a disaster, set up a company to manufacture the new product and so put Dundee on the food map of the world. Indeed, when the British Trade Mark Registry was set up in 1876, Keiller's Dundee Orange Marmalade was one of the first products to be registered. Today, Keillers keeps up its Dundee tradition, with the world's largest and most modern marmalade manufacturing plant based in the city.

The Scots, however, were not satisfied with inventing marmalade: they had to

Marmalade, first produced in Dundee at the end of the 18th Century, by **James Keiller**—'Keiller's Dundee Orange Marmalade.
ack: City of Dundee District Council, Art Galleries and Museums Department..

develop it further. A Paisley grocer in the 1850's saw the wider commercial potential of his wife's home-made marmalade which he sold in his shop. Her marmalade was clear with shreds of orange peel throughout. He christened it "Golden Shred" and set out to market it to the breakfast tables of the world, initially in stone jars with parchment lids and later with paper wrappers right round the jar.

Kidneys and kippers may have given way to fruit juice and muesli on the British breakfast table but marmalade retains its traditional place.

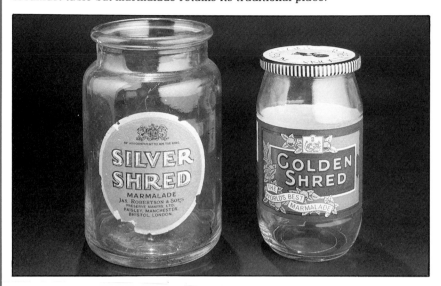

Marmalade 1850s Golden Shred.
ack: Paisley Museum and Art Gallery.

Cotton sewing thread: **James and Patrick Clark.**
Cotton reels: **J and J Clark.**
ack: Paisley Museum and Art Gallery.

James Clerk Maxwell first colour photograph.
ack: Trustees of the Science Museum, London.

Domestic Inventions

The Thermos flask: **Sir James Dewar.**
The kaleidoscope: **Sir David Brewster.**
The colour photograph: **James Clerk Maxwell.**
The rotary lawnmower: **David Cockburn.**
Cotton sewing thread: **James and Patrick Clark.**
Cotton reels: **J and J Clark.**
Canned salmon in the U.K.: **John Moir of Aberdeen.**
Rubber Wellington boots: **North British Rubber Company**
The Yule-tide greetings card: **Charles Drummond.**
The Milk Bar: **William Harley.**
The grand piano: **John Broadwood.**
The handkerchief: first manufactured in the U.K. in Paisley.
The chimney cowl: **James Anderson.**
The electric clock: **Alexander Bain.**
The piano pedal: **John Broadwood.**
Fingerprinting: **Henry Faulds.**
The Kola drink: a Scottish soft drinks manufacturer.
Lime juice as a soft drink: **Lachlan Rose.**
Marmalade: **Mrs. Keiller.**
Bovril: **James Johnstone.**
Continuous electric light: **James Bowman Lindsay.**
The waterproof: **Charles Macintosh.**
Cornflour: **John Polson.**
The self-acting fountain pen: **Robert Thomson.**

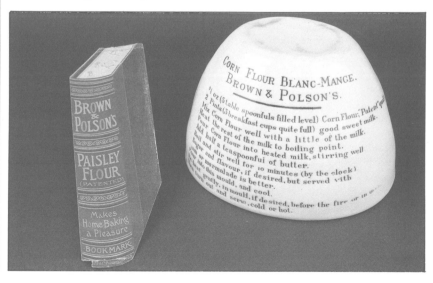

Cornflour: **John Polson.**
ack: Paisley Museum and Art Gallery.

The Scot Abroad

DAVID LIVINGSTONE

*"To begin the world again, anew, in a
new corner of it"*
Flora Macdonald

The Scot Abroad

Having protected Prince Charles Edward in his last days in Scotland, after the collapse of the Jacobite rebellion at Culloden, Flora Macdonald sought refuge and a new life in the United States. Today, thousands of Americans flock to her native mountains in Skye to seek their roots: her clan, the Clan Donald has over 100,000 members throughout the world.

Refuge from political and religious oppression was just one of the many reasons the Scots have spread their influence so far and wide. There is an old saying that *"the Scot is never so much at home as when he is abroad"*. Scotland's very shape and size offers part of the explanation. The rough terrain and uncertain climate of the Highlands, for example, led many Scots over the centuries to turn their faces south, away from eking a meagre living from the hostile soil, to the cities of Glasgow and Edinburgh, to London and to the new opportunities of the United States, Canada, Australia and New Zealand.

This movement was accelerated after Culloden and the "Forty Five" Rebellion. Stern measures were taken to subdue the fighting spirit of the Clans. The new landowners saw the potential of the Highlands in terms of sheep rearing and deer stalking rather than people. For many the only salvation was the advertisement in the local press offering a cheap passage across the Atlantic. For some it was the road to prosperity and fame: for others, the struggle to survive in the Frontier backwoods was little different than the life they had left. Some did not survive the gruelling sea voyage, herded like cattle in the insanitary holds of cargo ships: some did not even get that far. The bell in the Bell Tower of Robert Owen's New Lanark industrial community is inscribed *"Haggers Town....Maryland, 1786"*. It belonged to would-be emigrants to the State of Maryland from Caithness who, becoming storm bound on their journey to the Atlantic port of Greenock, decided to seek work in New Lanark instead.

Scotland's size also dictated another important contact with the world — trade. From earliest times, Scotland has been an exporting nation and where its people traded, they also settled. As early as 1297, Sir William Wallace was writing to the Senate and Commoners of Lübeck and Hamburg thanking them for their *"friendly and helpful counsel"* to Scottish merchants and offering safe conduct to any of their merchants who might venture to a Scottish port. Today, 1500 Scots still live and work in Hamburg. There was also a vigorous interchange of trade with the Low Countries, France and Scandinavia: it was a Scot who built Norway's first shipyard. Trading communities were established in the main European centres. The Schotsehuizen at Veere, where a community of Scottish traders lived under the control of the Scottish Lord Conservator still stands today. The Royal Bachelors' Club in Gothenburg, the world's fifth oldest gentleman's club, and one of its most exclusive, was founded by a Scottish merchant. Poland also had a strong Scots trading community. It is estimated that 30,000 Scots were living and doing business there in the 17th century. They left their mark on the language: the word Scot in Polish means a commercial traveller and there is a Polish proverb *"as poor as a Scots pedlar's pack"*. Not all clearly, made their fortune!

As new trading opportunities opened up so were the Scots to be found. It was the Scottish King James VI who was the first royal personage to write to an Emperor of Japan. The ensuing trade agreement gave the Japanese their first glimpse of the Stuart tartan which was reproduced in Japan during the period. Many of the early Indian "Nabobs" were Scottish, and later it was the Scots Hugh Falconer of Forres and William Jameson of Leith who were largely responsible for the development of tea plantations in India. Many of the great trading houses of the Far East such as Jardine Mathieson were founded and are still largely run by Scots. Westwards, too, the Scots cast their eyes and saw gold in the sugar plantations of Jamaica and the tobacco fields of Virginia, in the forests of Canada and the prairies of the Mid West. During the period from 1821-1870, 63% of the

Members of the train crew and several passengers pose for a photograph taken in 1886 of a westbound Canadian Pacific Railway "Pacific Express".

ack: CP Rail

Canadian Pacific Railway—largely financed, designed and built by Scottish endeavour.
ack: Canada House, London.

In this somewhat informal photograph, taken soon after the famous Last Spike ceremony, a child believed to be the son of Canadian Pacific construction manager James Ross, performs a spike-driving ceremony of his own.
ack: CP Rail

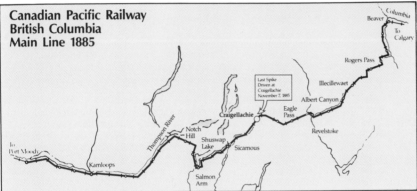

commissioned officers of the Hudson Bay Company were of Scots origin. Indeed, during the Klondike, Clyde ships were hired by the Canadian Pacific Railway Company to transport the miners to the Alaskan goldfields.

The Canadian Pacific Railway is itself a monument to the Scottish influence overseas, as it was largely financed, designed and built by Scottish endeavour. Scottish money and Scottish skills tended to follow in the path of Scottish trade. Scottish money lay behind three crucial stages of the development of the US economy in the 19th century: the ranching movement, mineral mining in the West and the opening up of the Great Plains to agriculture. One historian has attributed this to the "romantic, speculative inventiveness, crossed with the mentality of a chartered accountant" possessed by many Scots. Scottish investment in the United States reached a peak in the 1880's. The first large joint stock venture in cattle ranching in Texas, the Prairie Cattle Company Limited, was based in Edinburgh, although much of its capital came from Dundee, which invested £5 million in the US in the 1880's, an amount ten times that of the city's own real estate. Three-quarters of the overseas investment in US ranching came from Scotland. The provision of Scottish mortgage finance also played a key role in the development of US agriculture, where £8 million was invested in Texas mortgages alone in the 1880's. The rebuilding of Chicago after the fire of 1871 and the draining of the Sacramento swampland in California are just two examples of US endeavour backed by Scottish capital.

Scottish skill as well as capital was and still is much sought after throughout the world in the establishment and development of new industries. The Scottish engineer was to be found in every port: universally known as 'Mac' he buffeted his way round the world in a Clyde built ship tending a Clyde built engine. Scottish shipbuilding expertise was exported to build the floating docks of Java and Saigon and further back to set up the forerunners of the great European shipyards of Götaverken Arendal (Sweden) and Wartsila (Finland). Much of the development of Japanese shipbuilding over the last century has been in Scottish hands. Many of Japan's shipbuilders and naval architects were trained on the Clyde and the first Professor of Naval Architecture at Tokyo University was naturally a Glasgow University graduate. Dundee, renowned worldwide for its "Jute, Jam and Journalism", exported its skills to develop the jute industry of Calcutta. At one time Dundee based companies operated 3,714 jute looms in India and also provided an eighth of the capital investment involved in the development of the industry.

The export of industrial skills was a major underlying factor in much of the late 19th century Scottish emigration to North America. Five thousand Scottish Mormon miners emigrated to Utah from a mixture of economic and religious

Overseas trade shipping list.
ack: People's Palace Museum, Glasgow.

The Scot Abroad

motives and developed the mining industry there. The US thread making industry owes its development almost exclusively to Scots. Banking and business practice in Canada were largely modelled on the Scottish pattern and Scots were in the forefront of the development of the fur industry, timber, mining and civil engineering. Even in the most hostile of environments such as the whaling stations of the Antarctic and the frozen wastes of Siberia, Scottish enterprise flourished in outposts of companies such as Christian Salvesen of Edinburgh, at one time the world's largest whaling company, and the Glasgow engineering giant, William Beardmore.

David Livingstone at the Royal Geographical Society Picnic Party, Bath, 1864.

The impetus for emigration thus came as a result of political and religious oppression, trading opportunities or simply the spirit of adventure. This spirit of adventure must partially explain the Scottish contribution to exploration of the world's wild places. Why else did Mungo Park forsake the comforts of a Borders medical practice to explore the reaches of the Niger, or John Muir the early-to-bed routine of his East Lothian childhood to walk thousands of miles in the American hinterland? Was David Livingstone, the first white man to see what he christened the Victoria Falls, motivated by a missionary zeal to convert the natives to Christianity or did this simply provide the cloak of respectability to his basic desire for adventure? Whatever the reason, Scots influence followed in Livingstone's wake. Medical and teaching missions were set up in the area, which now forms part of Malawi. Scots businessmen formed the African Lakes Corporation in 1878 to improve communications and trade and to set up tobacco and tea plantations. The combined pressures from trade and mission soon persuaded the British Government to set up a Protectorate. The present President of Malawi, Hastings Banda, continues in the Scottish tradition as a graduate of the University of Edinburgh and an Elder of the Church of Scotland. This pattern of exploration, leading to trade, leading to settlement, is a common thread among many Scottish ventures overseas. Perhaps the spirit of adventure has been passed on today in the pursuit of the deepest recesses of space. John Glenn, Neil Armstrong, Alan Bean and Bruce McCandless all claim Scottish roots.

What sort of mark have the Scots left on the places that they settled? Their influence ranges from Mount Erebus in the Antarctic named after the ship of the

Scots explorer Sir James Ross to at least thirteen Presidents of the United States with some Scots blood in their veins. Communities, place names, institutions, and, most important of all, people, all bear the Scottish imprint—from the first non-Hispanic settler in California to the present Chief of the Creek Indians . . . from the founder of the New York Herald to the proprietor of Forbes Magazine . . . from the founder of the Banque Nationale to the present Chairman of Dalgety Inc . . . from the first Governor of the State of New Jersey to the first Prime Minister of Canada.

It is not possible to estimate how many people in the world today trace their ancestry back to Scotland. The popularity of Highland Games in places as far apart as Japan and Grandfather Mountain, North Carolina, the thousands of flourishing Burns Clubs and Caledonian Societies around the world, the countless golf clubs of which those in the US alone would cover a four and a half mile wide strip from one end of Scotland to the other—all are outward indications of the enduring Scottish influence. Some pointers to the size of the Scottish influence worldwide are provided by statistics: Scots form the third largest ethnic group in Canada and the second largest West European ethnic group in the United States, with 25,000 tracing their origin to pre-Revolutionary times. One in ten Australians has a Scottish surname.

Surnames provide a clue not only in the newer areas of Scots emigration but in Europe too. The name of one of Italy's leading aristocratic families is Scotti, tracing its history back to a Scot, William Douglas, who served under Charlemagne against the Lombards in the 9th century, and stayed on. The Scots role as mercenaries in the battlefields of Europe partly contributed to the existence of surnames today, with Stuarts and Colquhouns in Sweden, Drummonds, Crawfords and Moncrieffs in France and Taits, Ramsays, Mackays and MacKinnons in Finland. A quick glance at an atlas of the United States shows the wealth of cities and counties called after Scots or Scottish placenames. Names such as Highland Hills, Donaldsonville, Lennox, McIntyre and Stewart in Georgia reflect the number of Highlanders who served in the border defences against the Spanish in the 18th century. Even the maps of the original Colonies reflect pockets of Scottish immigration, in Massachusetts where granite quarriers were brought over from Aberdeen to work the local quarries, and in Carolina, where Highlanders, fleeing from the aftermath of the Jacobite rebellions, set up a Gaelic speaking community. One Highland emigrant, on arrival at Wilmington, was amazed to hear two blacks speaking Gaelic. The Highland community still flourishes today although the speaking of Gaelic has died out.

One instance will suffice to illustrate the prevalence of Scottish names. There are fourteen Aberdeens worldwide, seven of which are in the United States with others in Hong Kong, Canada, Australia, South Africa, Sierra Leone and Sri Lanka. To confuse matters further, Aberdeen, Mississippi, was previously called Dundee: like Aberdeen, Ohio, it was founded by a Scot. While Aberdeen, Scotland describes itself as "Europe's oil capital", another Aberdeen has adopted the motto "heart of Idaho's potato country". The traffic in names, however, is two way: Scotland itself boasts a Houston, a Waterloo and a Moscow.

Scots did not only give their names to places, but also to institutions such as McGill and Dalhousie Universities in Canada. The former was set up in 1829 from a bequest in the will of James McGill, a wealthy Glasgow born fur trader: its medical school was founded by four graduates from Scottish Universities, two of whom were native Scots. Montreal's main teaching hospital was financed by the benefactions of Donald Smith from Moray who rose from clerk in the Hudson Bay Company to the company's top position in North America. It is a reflection of the importance that Scots place on education that Scots are associated with the foundation of so many educational institutions; William and Mary, Calcutta University, Adelaide, the medical schools of Melbourne and Sydney, the first three Universities in India, Breadwinners College . . . It was also a Scot, John Witherspoon, the only cleric to sign the Declaration of Independence, who developed Princeton from a local Presbyterian college to one of the top three American Universities. Many overseas Universities modelled themselves on Edinburgh, some indeed literally. The teaching hospital in Montreal was built from the same architectural plans as Edinburgh's Royal Infirmary. Possibly the best known benefactor of all time, celebrated in the name of libraries in every state in the USA, and in many countries throughout the world, and celebrated in the many educational grants and scholarships that bear his name, is the Dunfermline weaver's son, Andrew Carnegie.

Of the many Scots who have played key roles, over the centuries, in the public stage of the world as prime ministers, as presidents, as admirals and generals, as bankers and industrialists, as doctors and scientists, it is impossible to do justice. Their biographies would fill a library. Taking the United States alone, thirty-five US Supreme Court Justices including John Marshall, arguably the greatest of them all, half of the Secretaries of the US Treasury, more than one hundred State Governors, nine of Washington's brigadier generals and nine of the signatories of the Declaration of Independence were all of Scots origin. Scots have founded the navies of Russia, Japan, Chile and the United States. They have shaped the state education system of India, the banking system of Canada and the legal system of several States of America. The Scots inventive streak has been handed on to their sons and daughters overseas in the discovery of insulin and chloroform, the telegraph and the phonograph, the splitting of the atom and telegraphy. The creative streak comes through in authors like Henry James and Edgar Allan Poe, in entertainers like Isadora Duncan and Hoagy Carmichael and in the Hollywood stardom of Joan Crawford, Sean Connery and David Niven.

Woodrow Wilson, once said: *"Every line of strength in American history is a line coloured with Scottish blood"*. It still runs true today.

The following lists include Scots who made their mark overseas and some well-known names who claimed to have Scots blood in their veins.

Great Scots in Europe

Charles Edward Stuart "Bonnie Prince Charlie" was born and died in Rome.
Daniel Home. *1833-86*: the Uri Geller of 19th century Europe. Gave performances to the Tsar of Russia and the Emperor Napoleon.
Edward Grieg: the Norwegian composer, descended from an Aberdeen emigrant.
Alexander Keiller. *b. 1804*: founded the Swedish shipyard from which Götaverken Arendal, one of Europe's top shipyards , is a direct descendant.
James Polwarth: painted the banner of Joan of Arc.
Mary Gardon: prima donna with the Opéra Comique de Paris.
Thomas Blaike: laid out the gardens at Bagatelle, and later Malmaison for the Empress Josephine.
Lord Henry Brougham: made Cannes a fashionable resort.
The Empress Eugenie: the last French Empress had a Scots mother and was descended from Robert the Bruce.
President de Gaulle: a far off descendant of an old Scots family.
Peter the Great.
William Davidson. *1593-1669*: the first Professor of Chemistry in France.
Donizetti: the Italian operatic composer.
Karl Marx's mother-in-law was Scottish, Jeannie Wishart.
Immanuel Kant: German philosopher believed himself to be of Scots extraction.
Lermontov: the Russian national poet.
St. Patrick: legend has it that he was born in the West of Scotland.
Eric Satie: French composer.

Great Scots in the United States

David Brodie Mitchell. *1766-1837*: Governor of Georgia.
Thomas Moonlight. *1833-1899*: Governor of Wyoming.
Alexander McDougall. *1731-86*: Member of the Continental Congress. Called the *"Wilkes of America"*.
Alexander McGraw. *1831-1905*: bridge builder who erected the pedestal of the Statue of Liberty.
Gabriel Johnston. *1699-1752*: Governor of North Carolina.
Thomas Leiper. *1745-1825*: Director of the Bank of the US and founder of the Franklin Institute in Philadelphia.
Charles Lockhart. *1818-1905*: President of Standard Oil.
Lawrie Walker. *1784-1868*: Secretary of the US Senate.
Samuel Johnston. *1733-1816*: Member of the Continental Congress and US Senator.
Sir William Keith. *1680-1749*: Governor of Pennsylvania and Delaware and Surveyor General for the Southern Colonies.
James Wilson. *1836-1920*: Secretary of Agriculture.
Alexander Hewat. *1745-1829*: wrote the first history of South Carolina.
James Halley. *1854-1920*: founder and first President of the First National Bank, Rapid City.
Grant Thorburn. *1773-1863*: ran first large American seed business and produced the first seed catalogue.
Andrew St. Clair. *1734-1818*: Governor of the North West Territories and one of the founders of the Pittsburgh iron industry.
William Addison Phillips: Commander of the Cherokee Indian Regiment in the Civil War and founder of the city of Salina, Kansas.
William Wilson. *1862-1934*: Secretary for Labour from *1913-21*.
John Paul Jones. *b. 1747*: Father of the American navy.
Allan Pinkerton: founder of the Pinkerton Detective Agency.
John Muir. *b. 1838*: Father of the conservation movement and founder of Yellowstone National Park.
Alexander Wilson: *1766-1813*: pioneer American ornithologist.
Samuel Wilson: the original Uncle Sam.

Gilbert Stuart: portrait painter.

John Mackintosh: developer of the Mackintosh red apple.

George Walter: pointed out to Washington the advantages of the site that was to become the national capital.

George Smith: founder of the first bank in Chicago.

Joseph Henry: the first Director of the Smithsonian Institution and developer of the theories of self-induction and the induction of currents.

Dr. John Stevenson: known as *"the American Romulus"* founded Baltimore. The town was laid out by fellow Scot, **George Buchanan.**

Henry Chisholm: the *"Father of Cleveland"* who introduced steelmaking to the city.

General John Forbes. *b. 1710:* founded the city of Pittsburg.

Alexander Steel Graham. *b. 1917:* creator of the Fred Bassett cartoon strip.

Andrew Carnegie. *1835-1919:* multi-millionaire philanthropist.

Robert Smith. *1722-77:* designed most of the Colonial buildings of Philadelphia including Franklin's house.

Alexander Mitchell: late 19th century President of the Chicago, Milwaukee, St. Paul and Pacific Railway.

John McLaren. *1846-1943:* created El Camino Real and Golden Gate Point Park in San Francisco.

William Drummond: first Governor of North Carolina.

Sir Alexander Cumming. *b. 1690:* elected Chief and Lawgiver of the Cherokee in 1730.

Adlai Stevenson: U.S. representative at the 1945 UN Assembly.

John McKenzie. *1763-1823:* founder of Chicago.

James Robertson. *1742-1804:* founder of Nashville, Tennessee.

Rev. James Blair. *1656-1743:* founder of William and Mary College.

Alexander Spotswood. *1676-1749:* Governor of Virginia. Encouraged the development of the tobacco industry.

Flora MacDonald: protector of Prince Charles Edward. Emigrated to the US and was present at the Cross Creek Rising.

Charles Thomson: author of the Declaration of Independence.

Richard Oswald: negotiated the peace treaty at the end of the War of Independence.

Tom Watson: four times winner of the Open Golf Tournament.

James Bowie: the American Scout who gave his name to the Bowie knife.

Andrew Hamilton: organised the first postal service in the American colonies.

John Marshall: arguably the greatest of all US Chief Justices.

James Pollock. *1810-90:* responsible for putting *"In God we Trust"* on the US coinage.

Dr. Archibald Bruce. *1777-1818:* first scientific mineralogist in the US.

Charles Wilson: founder of Holiday Inns.

James Wilson. *1742-98:* signatory to the Declaration of Independence.

Harry Hopkins: political adviser to President Roosevelt.

Russell Bean: the first white child to be born in Texas.

Dr. John Stevenson.

Great Scots in Canada

James Geddes. *1763-1838:* Chief Engineer on the Erie Canal.

George Forbes: Consulting engineer to the Niagara Falls Hydro-electric Scheme in *1892.*

Reginald Stewart. *1900-84:* founder of the Toronto Philharmonic Orchestra.

James Naismith. *1869-1931:* conceived the game of basketball.

Thomas Douglas, Earl of Selkirk. *1771-1820:* laid the foundations of Manitoba.

J K Galbraith: the economist.

Sir John A. McDonald. *1815-91:* first Prime Minister of the Dominion of Canada.

George Stephen. *1829-1921:* first President of the Canadian Pacific Railway Company.

Sir James Douglas. *1803-77:* first Governor of British Columbia.

Sir Hugh Allan. *1810-82:* co-founder of the Allan Shipping Line.

Sir George Ramsay. *1770-1838:* Lt. Governor of Nova Scotia.

Alexander Mackenzie. *1822-92:* second Prime Minister of Canada.

Lord Thomson of Fleet: newspaper proprietor.

Donald McGill. *1875-1940:* the author, was also Governor General of Canada.

Max Aitken, Lord Beaverbrook. *1879-1964:* the multi-millionaire newspaper proprietor.

John Galt. *1779-1839:* the novelist. As Secretary of the Canada Company opened up the area between Lakes Huron and Erie and founded the city of Guelph.

Sandford Fleming. *1827-1915:* a railway engineer, he also designed Canada's first stamp, the threepenny beaver, and played a major part in setting world time zones.

Great Scots worldwide

Hugh Falconer *1806-65* and **William Jamieson:** responsible for the development of tea plantations in India.

The Scot Abroad

Lord Maclehose of Beoch: Governor and Commander-in-Chief of Hong Kong. *1971-82.*

Lord Hopetoun: first Governor-General of Australia.

Thomas Sutherland. first Chairman of the Hong Kong Dockyard Company.

Sir James Carnhill. *1851-1926:* the first student of his college for Chinese medical students in Hong Kong, later became the first President of the Chinese Republic.

Sir John Macarthur. *1767-1834:* established the Australian wool industry and planted the first vineyard.

Dame Nellie Melba: the operatic singer, who also lent her name to "peach melba".

Allan Octavian Hume: founder of the Indian Congress Party.

Mountstuart Elphinstone. *1779-1857:* founded the Indian State education system.

Lord Gladstone of Lanark: first Governor-General of South Africa.

Thomas Macaulay: originator of the Indian Penal Code.

William Kidston. *b. 1840:* founded Queensland University, Australia.

William Paterson. *1755-1800:* introduced the peach to New South Wales.

Sir William Cresswell. *1852-1933:* founder of the Australian navy.

George Boyle. *1746-81:* the first Briton to visit Tibet where he concluded a commercial treaty with the Panchen Lama.

Sir James Robertson. *1901-83:* first Governor-General of Nigeria.

Rev. Thomas Burns and **Capt. William Cargill:** in the 1840's established Otago and Dunedin, in New Zealand.

Lachlan Macquarie. *1761-1824:* as Governor, transformed New South Wales from a penal colony.

Catherine Spence. *1825-1910:* Australia's first woman novelist.

James Chisholm: ran the first saloon in Sydney, called the Thistle Tavern.

Samuel Laing: India's first Finance Minister.

Brisbane, Australia.
ack: The Australian Information Service, London.

The Ross Sea.
The 'Discovery' in pack ice in the Ross Sea, Antarctica.
ack: Royal Geographical Society.

Places named after Scots

Craigsville, New York.
Hector's Pass, Rocky Mountains.
The Falkland Islands.
McAlisterville, Pennsylvania.
The Frazer River, Canada.
Brisbane, Australia.
Beardmoreland, USSR.
The Beardmore Glacier, Antarctica.
The Heights of Abraham, Canada.
Muir Woods, California.
The Mackenzie River, Canada.
The Ross Sea, Antarctica.
Macquarie Straits, south of New Zealand.
Mount Hooker, Rocky Mountains.
Mount Geikie, Rocky Mountains.
Cape Brewster, Greenland.
Jameson Land, Greenland.
Braidwood, Illinois.
Galt, Canada.
Livingstone, Malawi.

The Falkland Islands.
Stanley Harbour, 1856.
ack: BBC Hulton Picture Library, London.

The inventive Scots blood will out

The tubular wheeled tyre.
Insulin.
The telephone.
Stereotyping.
Anaesthesia.
Morse code.
Telegraphy.
The steamboat.
The reaper.
Electric light.
The brassiere.
Chloroform.
Shorthand.
Canada dry.
Splitting of the atom.
Vacuum gauge.
The electric pen.
The thermionic valve.
The electron.
The refrigerator.

Telephone.
ack: Telecom Technology Showcase, London.

Discovery of the anaesthetic effect of chloroform, invented by a fellow Scot in the US, by **Sir James Young Simpson**, **Dr Thomas Keith** and **Dr James Matthews Duncan**, on 4 November 1857.
ack: Wellcome Institute Library, London.

Stereographer's tool kit.
ack: The People's Palace Museum, Glasgow.

Bell's reaper.
ack: Trustees of the Science Museum, London.

An early steamboat on the River Clyde off Dumbarton Rock in the 1820's.
ack: Museum of Transport, Glasgow.

US Presidents with Scots blood in their veins

William McKinlay
Andrew Jackson
Theodore Roosevelt
Woodrow Wilson
James Polk
Ulysses Grant
Lyndon Johnson
Ronald Reagan
Thomas Jefferson
James Munroe
Andrew Hamilton
James Buchanan
Andrew Johnson

Theodore Roosevelt (1858-1919).
ack: BBC Hulton Picture Library, London.

Lyndon Johnson (1908-1973).
36th President of the United States.
ack: BBC Hulton Picture Library, London.

Woodrow Wilson (1856-1924).
ack: BBC Hulton Picture Library, London.

84

Ronald Reagan.
Above left: Inside the Capitol Rotunda, President Reagan is sworn in by Chief Justice Warren E Burger 21 January 1985.
Above right: President and Mrs Reagan arrive with their dog, Lucky, on the south lawn of the White House from Camp David.
ack: BBC Hulton Picture Library, London.

Scottish American links

The first overseas Anglican bishop, **Samuel Seabury** was consecrated Bishop of Connecticut at Aberdeen in *1784.*

Madeline Smith, the central figure, in what is probably the most famous Victorian murder case, spent her last years in the United States.

Elizabeth Blackwell, the first American woman doctor retired to Dunoon in Argyllshire where she is buried.

The first Mayor of Buffalo is buried in Edinburgh.

Robert Burns wrote a poem on the American War of Independence *"An Ode for General Washington's Birthday".*

There is a replica of **Burns'** cottage in Atlanta, Georgia.

Thomas Jefferson, James Madison and **John Marshall** all had Scottish school teachers.

Madeleine Smith
ack: Glasgow Herald and Evening Times.

Carpet in the White House ordered from Templeton's on behalf of Mrs Lincoln.

The carpet is an ingenious piece of work, not because of its rich quality or exquisite design, but because of the fact that it is in one piece, and covers a floor measuring 100 feet long and 48 feet wide.

ack: White House Collection.

The Chief of the Cree Indian nation bears the name **McIntosh,** dating back to the days when a Highlander married a Princess of the tribe.

The legislation of several states in the US is modelled directly on Scots Law.

Mrs Abraham Lincoln carpeted the White House from the Glasgow firm of **Templeton's.** The bill, however, was not settled until the end of the 19th century.

The best oak for making casks to store Scotch whisky is the American white oak.

The first iron vessel to sail in US waters, "John Randolph" was shipped out to Savannah in sections from the Glasgow shipyard of **William Laird.**

The American naturalist **Audubon** had the plates for his books processed in Edinburgh because of its reputation for fine printing.

Scottish European links

A ceiling in the Villa Borghese in Rome was painted by the Scots neo-classical painter, **Gavin Hamilton.**

George Buchanan. *1506-82:* The Scots scholar and poet taught the French philosopher, Montaigne.

Until the Middle Ages the Western Isles, Orkney and Shetland belonged to Norway.

The inhabitants of Bergen in Norway often wear Balmoral bonnets, first introduced by Scottish sailors over 400 years ago.

James Boswell, the 18th century Scots biographer, was a student at the University of Utrecht, as was his father and grandfather.

The strong cultural link between France and Scotland, traditionally allies against the English in the Middle Ages, is shown in the similarity of many dialect words such as bon/bonnie, brave/braw, dur/dour, se facher/fash and assiette/ashet.

The royal palace in Amsterdam was built about *1680* by the Scots **Earl of Kincardine,** using Scottish stone.

When Joan of Arc entered Orleans it was to the tune *"L'Air des Soldats de Robert Bruce".* **Robert Burns** put words to the music to celebrate the Fall of the Bastille.

Spain's first football club was set up by Scottish lace workers who worked in the Spanish subsidiary of a Scots lace weaving company.

The Vatican's Palatinate Collection is based on the library drawn up by the Scot, **Henry Scrimgeour,** for the German banking family, the Fuggers.

Sir Arthur Conan Doyle, the Scots author, introduced Norwegian skiing to Switzerland.

Louis Pasteur spent some time in Younger's brewery in Edinburgh to further his studies on the fermentation process.

The Continuing
Tradition of Innovation

SCINTILLATION COUNTER

*"It has taken great men to discover
simple things."*
Wentworth D'Arcy Thomson

The Continuing Tradition of Innovation

It is only time that will separate the true innovations that shape the future from the bright ideas of today, that will distinguish the leap in the dark from the glitter of novelty. Scots still maintain that unique blend of idealism, tempered with practicality, that has characterised their achievements of the past three hundred years. They still place great emphasis on the value of education. Scotland today produces more graduates per head of population than any other country in Western Europe. The four traditional seats of learning whose portals have welcomed some of Scotland's greatest innovators have been joined by four younger Universities, two of which, as technological universities, expressly carry on the traditional bias of Scottish education towards the practical sciences. The venerable facades of the older Universities shelter research into artificial intelligence and laser technology, while the medical schools continue to train the world's doctors.

In some ways the days of the individual innovator are over. Figures like James Syme and Joseph Black were lionised by their contemporaries and their personal contribution to their chosen discipline has stood the test of centuries. It is more difficult to envisage their equivalents today where television leads to instant fame and where the pace of technology is such that the contribution of the individual tends to be a piece in an ever more complex jigsaw.

The closeness of the scientific community in 18th and 19th century Scotland is in some ways a surprising one, given the limitations of the speed of travel and of communications. Men like Cullen and Kelvin were generalists, their interests covering a very wide range of disciplines. It was common for a medical professor to lecture in chemistry or for a physicist to have research interests in engineering. Today, the much greater degree of specialisation within disciplines, the splitting of a subject into its many component parts and the consequent rise of the expert have ironically limited the wider horizons of science and the confidence to range widely across disciplines.

As a result of the communications revolution of the 20th century, research has become a very different activity. In some ways it is a much smaller world with instant access to research results through on-line databases and computer links. Contact with fellow specialists worldwide is only a telephone call away and the universal flow of ideas is sustained through international congresses and seminars. It has led to the development of collaborative research. A European wide research programme towards the development of an optical computer is being co-directed from the Physics Department of Heriot-Watt University in Edinburgh, while St Andrews physicists collaborate with their Chinese counterparts towards the greater understanding of solar flares.

The benefits of international co-operation are many but the sheer scale of the research tends to mask the contribution of the individual researcher. Archibald Couper died, his spirit broken after Kekule gained the credit for Couper's discovery that carbon is quadrivalent and can form linkages with other carbon atoms. The professor to whom Couper sent his results did not have the nerve to publish such a novel set of ideas. Today partly due to the much wider access to information, teams of researchers throughout the world race to become the first to publish.

Despite the vastly increased channels of communication, the work of the individual inventor has to some extent gone underground. The growth of company based research, the need for secrecy to maintain competitiveness, the increasing complexity of patent law and intellectual property rights all militate against knowledge of individual researchers and innovators. In many ways, a Brewster or a Nasmyth would envy the present level of commercial confidentiality: like many inventors before, and since, they both expended considerable energy and anxiety over imitators of their ideas. The losers are the future generations who can know less of the individuals behind the inventions, their hopes and aspirations, their failures and successes.

The passage of time is still the major factor in the identification of the true innovators of today. Time has to pass to distinguish a significant advance from a mistaken lead. In his day, the Scot who devised a machine to be driven by mouse power no doubt thought that he had solved the energy crisis! Often the significance of an advance in man's knowledge of the world may not be realised at the time: it is only recently that scientists have ceased to scoff at the theory of the Scotsman, James Croll, who postulated that cosmic influences were responsible for warm and cold ages on a global scale, not simply in particular areas. Work of scientists may be dusted down after the lapse of centuries as their theories gain renewed significance in the pursuit of new technologies. John Scott Russell's discovery of the soliton was a result of his interest in making ships travel faster through water: it is also central to the behaviour of light in optical fibres. Some inventions may be too costly to be exploited at the time. It was the cost of india rubber that led to Thomson's tyre being discarded: it was only when its cost came down that Dunlop had the opportunity to reinvent the wheel! Some inventions or ideas may simply be too far ahead of their time to be adopted. It was many years before surgeons abandoned their established, unhygienic practices in favour of Lister's carbolic spray.

Seabug, a seabed crawler for inspecting North Sea
oil pipelines (First produced in 1978 in Aberdeen, by
the UDI Group).
ack: UDI, Aberdeen.

It is nonetheless intriguing to speculate as to Scotland's future contribution to innovation, to gaze into the crystal ball of invention and try to spot the image of a future Maxwell. Certain recent Scottish innovations have already established themselves in the history of innovation: the pregnancy scanner, interferon, the scintillation counter. Others have earned a place in the commercial marketplace. The technology of the Seabug, a seabed crawler, has proved its indispensability in inspecting and maintaining the pipelines that carry North Sea oil to its many destinations. Scottish made Soy sauce, a world first in applying biotechnology to a centuries old product, may one day take its place on the dinner tables of the world. Others are emerging from the chrysallis of academic research to test their wings in the wider world: ways of controlling the release of drugs into the body; NMR scanning techniques; a furrowed or "sulcated" spring which has significant potential in solving many of today's engineering problems; a vaccine against the herpes virus.

Scots are carrying out their traditional role of innovation in the fight against disease. Having successfully isolated the leukaemia virus in cats, researchers in Glasgow are working towards solving the puzzle of the disease in humans. St Andrews University is home to one of the world's thirty-four Cancer Research Workshops and is working with the aid of computer technology to investigate the fundamental structural differences between healthy and cancerous cells. Edinburgh University has launched a major attack on the prevention of crippling diseases such as spina biffida and cystic fibrosis through screening of the unborn child; while Strathclyde University turns its engineering expertise to easing the pains of old age through the development of sophisticated artificial joints.

Scots have adopted the legacy of electronics left to them by James Clerk Maxwell in the same way as they once followed through the revolutionary implications of James Watt's steam engine. Universities and companies work hand in hand in advancing the technologies involved in semiconductors, optoelectronics and artificial intelligence. The world's first silicon compiler was developed in Edinburgh as was the world's first optical amplifier. Often in their quest to extend the frontiers of knowledge even further, Scots turn back to the legacy of their forefathers. Strathclyde University researchers are working on the techniques of operating silicon chips at the temperature of liquid helium. In this they are simply following in the tradition of James Dewar and William Ramsay.

If this book is rewritten a hundred years on, who knows what names may appear. Only time has the answer.

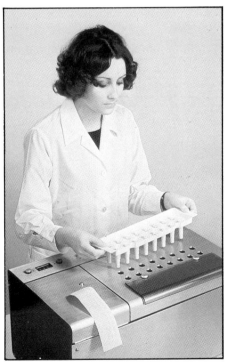

Scintillation counter.
The NE1600 multi-detector scintillation counter for
Radio-Immunoassay manufactured by Nuclear
Enterprises of Edinburgh.
ack: Nuclear Enterprises Limited, Reading.

A Scots Hotch Potch

BUSIEST TRAMWAY CROSSING IN THE WORLD

A Scots Hotch Potch

The following lists are intended simply to give a flavour of the variety of the Scottish contribution.

Busiest tramway crossing in the world—Jamaica Street/Renfield Street/Argyle Street in Glasgow.
1930

ack: T & R Annan and Sons Limited.

Society Firsts

The first agricultural society in the UK: The Honourable Society of Improvers of the Knowledge of Agriculture in Scotland, *1723*.

The first music society in the UK: The Edinburgh Music Society, *1728*.

The first medical society in the UK: The Society for the Improvement of Medical Knowledge, *1737*.

The first recorded curling club: the Muthill Curling Society, *1789*.

The world's first golf club: the Honourable Society of Edinburgh Golfers, *1764*.

The world's first chemical society, *1840*.

The world's first amateur photographic society: Calotype Club, founded in Edinburgh in *1842*.

The world's first Indian Association, *1883*.

The world's first banking professional body: The Institute of Bankers, dating from *1875*.

The American Political Science Association.

The Society of American Artists.

The Cavendish Society.

Institute of Accountants.

British Association for the Advancement of Science.

The Chemical Society.

The Institute of Landscape Architects (now The Landscape Institute).

Institution of Civil Engineers.

Scottish Biggest and Best

Tallest trees in Great Britain: Strone Gardens, Cairndow, near Inveraray, and The Hermitage, Perth.

Once the busiest tramway crossing in the world: Jamaica Street/Renfield Street, Glasgow.

The longest swing bridge in Europe: the Kincardine Bridge over the Forth.

The world's shortest scheduled air route: lasting two minutes between Westray and Papa Westray in Orkney.

Largest man-made hole in Europe: Westfield, Fife.

The tallest hedge in the world: Meikleour beech hedge, Perthshire.

The oldest tree in Britain: Fortingall, Perthshire.

The world's largest dock gate: Nigg, Ross and Cromarty.

The largest academic library building in Europe: Edinburgh.

The world's oldest rock: Archean Gneiss, Lewis.

The longest series of accurate weather records: Edinburgh.

The world's largest passenger liner: the "Queen Elizabeth", *1934*, built on the Clyde.

The largest collection of rhododendrons in the world: Royal Botanical Gardens, Edinburgh.

The world's hardest biscuit: Bickiepegs on which Royalty have cut their teeth.

The world's largest arts festival: Edinburgh.

The longest swing bridge in Europe, Kincardine Bridge, over the Forth (built 1936).
ack: Royal Commission on Ancient Monuments, Scotland.

Queen Mary.
ack: Glasgow Room, Mitchell Library, Glasgow.

Songs with a Scots Composer

"Oh Susannah" and "Jeannie with the Light Brown Hair", composed by Stephen Foster, of Scots descent.

"The Maple Leaf", composed by Alexander Muir, born in Scotland.

"Waltzing Matilda".

"Advance Australia Fair".

"Holar uho Hikari" (Japanese children's song sung to the tune of "Auld Lang Syne").

"Ye Mariners of England".

"Abide with Me".

Journals and newspapers founded by Scots

The American Journal of Education.

The Scots Farmer: the first agricultural journal in the U.K.

The Municipal Journal.

Forbes Magazine.

The New York Tribune.

The Boston Chronicle.

The New York Herald.

The Toronto Globe.

Mind.

The Economist.

The Scots Magazine: the oldest surviving magazine in the U.K.

The Glasgow Herald: the oldest national daily newspaper in the English speaking world.

The Spectator.

The Political Quarterly.

The Edinburgh Medical Journal: the oldest medical journal in the U.K.

Above: The Economist (front page of an early issue).
ack: The Mitchell Library, Glasgow.

Far left: The Scots Magazine, the oldest surviving magazine in the UK.
ack: The Scots Magazine.

Above left: The Glasgow Herald—the oldest national daily newspaper in the English-speaking world. *1783.*
ack: Glasgow Herald and Evening Times.

Left: Forbes Magazine *(1917).*
Malcolm S Forbes, current Chairman and Editor-in-Chief. (Behind is painting of his father, B C Forbes, founder of the magazine).
ack: Barry McKinley.

The Natural Kingdom discovered by Scots

The genus Hopea.

The Gardenia.

Grant's Gazelle.

Thomson's Gazelle.

Sibbald's Rorqual: the blue whale.

The Douglas Spruce.

The lechwe: named by David Livingstone.

The nu-nu mouse: a hairless mouse, first bred in Glasgow, of great importance in medical research.

Scottish contribution to Civil Engineering/ Construction

The chain bridge over the Danube linking Buda and Pest.

The Gota Canal linking the Baltic with the North Sea, in Sweden.

The Canadian Pacific Railway.

The first railway line across the Alps.

The Pavlosk Palace for Catherine the Great.

Britain's longest acqueduct, The Pontcysyllte in Wales.

St. Katherine's Dock, London.

The world's first wrought iron girder bridge, Glasgow.

The first suspension bridge in the UK: the Union Suspension Bridge over the Tweed.

The Forth Railway Bridge.

The steelwork of Tower Bridge, London.

The El Giza bridge across the Nile at Cairo.

Waterloo Bridge.

The principle of box girders in bridge building, Glasgow.

Scottish Military Men

Lord Dowding: Leader of Fighter Command in the Second World War.

Earl Haig.

General Douglas MacArthur: Commander of the Combined Allied Forces in the South West Pacific: was the grandson of a Glaswegian.

Jacques Law. 1768-1828: Napoleon's aide-de-camp and Marechal of France.

General Charles Gordon. 1838-85: nicknamed "Chinese Gordon" unsuccessfully held Khartoum against the Mahdi.

Sir Charles James Napier. 1782-1853: responsible for the annexation of the Indian Province of Sind to Britain and, as Governor, for the development of Karachi.

William Keith, a native of Peterhead: became a Marshall in the army of Frederick the Great and became a close personal friend: in 1868 William I of Prussia presented a statue of him to his home town.

Forth Railway Bridge (from South).
ack: Royal Commission on Ancient Monuments, Scotland.

First suspension bridge in the UK—Union Suspension Bridge, over the Tweed (built by Samuel Brown— 1820).
ack: Royal Commission on Ancient Monuments, Scotland.

Thomas Bruce 7th Earl of Elgin: "rescued" what became known as the Elgin marbles from the Parthenon in 1803.

The Royal Scots: the oldest regiment in the world.

George, Earl of Orkney, and John, 2nd Duke of Argyll, were the first people to hold the newly created title of Field Marshall in 1736.

William McGonagall: claimed by many to be the world's worst poet.

Pontius Pilate: reputedly born in Scotland while his father was on military service.

Butch Cassidy: member of the Wild Bunch had a Scots mother.

The last person to be publicly hanged in Britain was a Glasgow Fenian, in 1868.

William Money: "the first outstanding eccentric of Los Angeles" who emigrated from Scotland in 1843. His interest in geology led him to the theory that underlying San Francisco the earth's crust was almost burnt out by subterranean fires and would break one day "spilling the ungodly city directly into the flaming cauldron of Hell".

Captain Kidd: the legendary pirate was born in Greenock around 1645.

Vice-President Aaron Burr: shot the former Secretary of the US Treasury, Alexander Hamilton, after a St. Andrews Society dinner in New York. Both were of Scots descent.

Henry Ford I (1863-1947).
ack: Ford of Europe Incorporated.

Top right: Trust House Forte. Sir Charles Forte at his office desk, picture of father on wall behind him.
Above: Lord Forte presents gifts to Lord Provost Gray of Glasgow at Pollock House.
ack: The Scotsman Publications Limited, Edinburgh.

Cunard (photo shows entire present fleet of Cunard vessels).
Left to right: Cunard Princess, Cunard Countess, Vistafjord, Sagafjord, Queen Elizabeth II.
ack: Cunard Line.

Companies founded by Scots

Macmillans: the Publishers.

ICI: the chemical multinational.

Ford Motor Corporation: Henry Ford came from Scots Irish stock.

The Bell Telephone Corporation: the US telephone corporation.

Dunlop: the tyre multinational.

Harvard University Press: the US academic publishers.

Cunard: the Queen of shipping.

Trust House Forte: the hotel group.

The Orient Line, now part of P and O: the shipping group.

Jardine Matheson: the Far East trading company.

The Burmah Oil Company: the oil multinational.

The Shore Porters Society of Aberdeen: the world's oldest documented company still trading.

Scots Politicians

John Glasier: Chairman of the Independent Labour Party 1900-3.

The Duchess of Atholl: the first Woman Conservative Minister.

Mary McArthur: the first woman to be adopted as a parliamentary candidate.

James Keir Hardie: first Leader of the Labour Party in Parliament.

Earl of Aberdeen: Victorian Prime Minister.

Ramsay Macdonald: Britain's first Labour Prime Minister.

Arthur Balfour: 20th century British Prime Minister.

Henry Campbell Bannerman: 20th century British Prime Minister.

Harold Macmillan: 20th century British Prime Minister.

Sir Alec Douglas Home: 20th century British Prime Minister.

Andrew Bonar Law: 20th century British Prime Minister.

J T Walton Newbold: returned for Motherwell in 1922 as the first Communist MP in Parliament.

Charles Jardine Don: the world's first Labour MP: served in the Victoria Legislative Assembly, Australia from 1859.

Andrew Dawson: the world's first Labour Prime Minister, in Australia in 1899. His administration only lasted one day.

Alexander Macdonald: the first working class MP in Britain.

R B Cunninghame Graham: the first Socialist MP in Britain.

Edwin Scrimgeour: in 1922 became Britain's first (and last) Prohibitionist MP.

Some Scots entertainers

Harry Lauder.
Charlton Heston.
Jack Buchanan.
Beryl Reid.
Tom Conti.
Isadora Duncan.
Robert Montgomery.
Hoagy Carmichael.
David Niven.
Sean Connery.
Mary Ure

Scottish books and bookmen

The first book to be translated from English into a foreign language.

The first comprehensive history of American literature was written by **Professor John Nichol** of Glasgow University in *1885*.

The author of the first U.S. Geological Survey, **William McClure** was born in Ayr in *1763*.

The first English Concordance to the Bible was compiled by **Alexander Conden,** *1701-70*.

Walter Scott is the world's first historical novelist.

The first editor of the Oxford English Dictionary was the Scot, **James Murray**.

The first edition of the Encyclopaedia Britannica was compiled, edited and printed in Edinburgh: *1768-81*.

The first English textbook on marine surveying: published by **Alexander Dalrymple** in *1771*.

The first treatise on coal: written by **George Sinclair** in *1672*.

"Liber Excertionum" was the first encyclopaedia to be compiled by a Briton: it was written at St. Victor's Abbey, Paris, by the Scots monk **Richard** around *1140*.

The world's first art book, published by **Sir William Stirling** in *1847*.

The world's most prolific gardening author, **John Claudius Loudon**.

The first monograph on the whale was written by **Robert Sibbald,** *1641-1722*.

The first textbook of surgery written in English, written by **Peter Lowe** in *1597*.

The first physical atlas in the U.K. was produced by the Edinburgh cartographers, **W and A K Johnston** in *1848*.

The first text to treat pathology as a subject was written by the Scots doctor, **Matthew Baillie,** *1761-1823*.

The first monograph on brain tumours: *1888*: **Frederick Bramwell**.

The first treatise on poisons in the English language: **Robert Christison,** *1797-1882*.

The first modern pharmacopoeia, the Materia Medica Catalogue of *1776*, was produced by **William Cullen**.

Sir Harry Lauder.
ack: The Sir Harry Lauder Society.

Sean Connery.
ack: BBC Hulton Picture Library, London.

David Niven.
ack: BBC Hulton Picture Library, London.

Sir Walter Scott *(right)* was the world's first historical novelist.
ack: National Galleries of Scotland, Edinburgh.

Encyclopædia Britannica;

OR, A

DICTIONARY

OF

ARTS and SCIENCES,

COMPILED UPON A NEW PLAN.

IN WHICH

The different SCIENCES and ARTS are digested into
distinct Treatises or Systems;

AND

The various TECHNICAL TERMS, &c. are explained as they occur
in the order of the Alphabet.

ILLUSTRATED WITH ONE HUNDRED AND SIXTY COPPERPLATES.

By a SOCIETY of GENTLEMEN in SCOTLAND.

IN THREE VOLUMES.

VOL. I.

EDINBURGH:

Printed for A. BELL and C. MACFARQUHAR;
And sold by COLIN MACFARQUHAR, at his Printing-office, Nicolfon-street.

M.DCC.LXXI.

Titlepage of the first edition of the Encyclopaedia Britannica, compiled, edited and printed in Edinburgh, titlepage.
ack: National Galleries of Scotland, Edinburgh.

Scottish books and bookmen (continued)

The first scientific textbook to be based on Newtonian theory was written by **David Gregory,** *1661-1710.*

The first authoritative text on tropical medicine was written by **James Lind,** *1716-92.*

The greatest exhortation to the Victorian virtues was **Samuel Smiles'** 'Self-help'.

The first systematic treatise on Chemistry, which, for example, showed letters to symbolise elements was written by the first Professor of Chemistry at Glasgow University, **Thomas Thomson,** *1773-1852.*

Published by Scots

The first complete English Bible in the US.

First edition of Tom Paine's "Common Sense".

The first Bible in raised type for the blind.

The first detective story to be published in the UK appeared in Chambers Edinburgh Journal, *1844.*

The first newspaper printed in North America.

The first newspaper printed in Illinois.

The first book to be written and printed in Los Angeles.

The first modern bookjacket.

The first coloured newspaper advertisement.

The first picture postcards in the UK.

The first postcard.

The Scots at war

The smokescreen: first suggested by **Archibald Cochrane,** 9th Earl of Dundonald. *1749-1831.*

Ballistics as an exact science: **Sir Andrew Noble.** *b. 1831.*

Shrapnel: first tested at the Carron Iron Works in *1784.*

Cordite: the explosive invented by **Sir James Dewar.** *1842-1923.*

The breech loading rifle: **Col. Patrick Ferguson.** *1744-80.*

The percussion lock: **Alexander Forsyth.** *1768-1843.*

The bolt action and magazine of the Lee-Enfield rifle: **James Lee.** *1831-1904.*

The carronade: **General Robert Melville.** *1723-1809.*

The aircraft carrier: **The Duke of Montrose.** *1878-1954.*

The Anderson air raid shelter: **Sir William Paterson.** *1874-1956.*

The gas mask: **John Stenhouse.** *1809-90.*

Industry Greats— at one time or another

Largest sulphuric acid plant in the world.

Largest producer of steam locomotives in Europe.

Largest manufacturer of fireclay products in the world.

The world's most successful oil field.

The largest shipping company in the world.

The largest whaling company in the world.

World's largest manufacturers of sugar refining machinery.

The world's largest bottle manufacturing complex.

Europe's most automated brewery.

The largest steel mill in Europe.

The longest natural gas liquids pipeline outside the U.S.

The world's largest stone working machine manufacturers.

The largest structural steelworks in Britain.

Britain's largest producer of alum, the mordaunt used in dyeing.

Men of mathematics

Principle of fractional indices: **Sir John Napier.** *1550-1617.*

Logarithms: **Sir John Napier.** *1550-1617.*

Rules for establishing the sections of prisms, cylinders and cylindroids: **Peter Nicholson.** *1765-1844.*

The Stirling Theorem: **James Stirling.** *1820-1909.*

The topology of knots: **P. G. Tait.** *1831-1901.*

The trigonometry of multiple angles: **Alexander Anderson.** *1582-1619.*

Foundations of modern algebra: **Duncan Gregory.** *1813-1844.*

Some of the principles of calculus: **James Gregory.** *1638-1675.*

McLaurin's Theorem: **Colin McLaurin.** *1698-1746.*

The theory of determinants: **Sir Thomas Muir.** *1844-1934.*

The decimal point: **Sir John Napier.** *1550-1617.*

Proof of the inverse square law of mechanics: **John Robison.** *1739-1805.*

Above right: Sherlock Holmes.
ack: The Stanley MacKenzie Collection.

Robinson Crusoe modelled on the real life adventures of Alexander Selkirk, the Fife castaway.
ack: The Mitchell Library, Glasgow.

Famous characters from Scottish fiction

Humphrey Clinker
Robinson Crusoe.
Rip Van Winkle.
Sherlock Holmes.
Moby Dick.
Dr. Jekyll.
Long John Silver.
Lucia di Lammermuir.
Wee Willie Winkie.
Goldilocks and the Three Bears.
*Frankenstein.
*Big Brother.
007.
Toad of Toad Hall.
Peter Pan.
Jean Brodie.
Don Juan

*written by non Scots in Scotland.

Long John Silver in "Treasure Island" by R L Stevenson.
ack: The Mitchell Library, Glasgow.

Ten Scots explorers

Sir Charles Wyville Thomson. *1830-82:* first person to explore the depths of the ocean.

James Bruce. *1730-94:* first European to discover the source of the Blue Nile.

Hugh Clapperton: crossed the Sahara and discovered Lake Chad in *1823.*

Alexander Mackenzie. *1767-1820:* first person to cross the American continent.

Dr. John Rae. *1813-93:* mapped the Northern coast of Canada.

Sir James Ross. *1800-62:* Antarctic explorer who discovered the world's most southerly volcanoes, Erebus and Terror.

Mungo Park. *1771-1806:* discovered most of the course of the Niger.

John McDowall Stuart. *1815-66:* first person to cross Australia from South to North.

David Livingstone. *1813-73:* the first white man to see Victoria Falls: discovered Lake Nyasa and explored long sections of the Zambezi.

James Grant, from Nairn, with John Speke was the first European to cross Equatorial Africa: they may also have discovered the source of the Nile in *1860-1,* although this claim was disputed by Sir Richard Burton.

John McDowall Stuart the first person to cross Australia from South to North.
ack: The John McDowall Stuart Museum, Dysart, Fife.

Scotland and the movies

The first advertising film, in *1897* was for Haig's Scotch Whisky.

The first inflight movie was based on Sir Arthur Conan Doyle's "The Lost World".

The first televised film in Britain was made by **John Logie Baird.** *1888-1946.*

One of the films in the first commercial film showing in *1884* was entitled: "Highland Fling".

The Scenic Director of MGM from *1939-1964* was the Scot, **George Gibson.**

John Grierson *1898-1972* was the founding father of the British documentary film movement and coined the word "documentary".

The first motion picture to involve the use of actors was "Mary, Queen of Scots". Shot in *1895.*

The first horror movie was based on **R L Stevenson's** "Dr Jekyll and Mr Hyde": *1908.*

The world's first Panorama, forerunner of the cinema, was created by **Robert Barker** in Edinburgh in *1784.*

Motion in pictures: **Sir David Brewster.** *1781-1868.*

The fixed focus pocket camera was invented by a Dundee scientific instrument maker, **George Loudon.** *1825-1912.*

The first colour photograph, appropriately of a tartan ribbon, was prepared by **James Clerk Maxwell.** *1831-79.*

The first film of a total eclipse of the sun: **Duke of Montrose.** *1878-1954.*

Scottish sporting firsts

First British Open Golf Tournament. *1861:* Paisley.

First Lacrosse Club in Great Britain. *1867:* Glasgow.

First person to adopt the "On your marks" position at the beginning of a race—the Maori runner with the splendidly Scots name of **Bobby MacDonald** at a Scottish athletics meeting in *1894.*

The modern rules of bowling: drawn up by **William Mitchell** in *1848.*

The Queensberry rules in boxing. **John Sholto Douglas** and **John Chalmers:** *1867.*

The rules of the game of rounders: Scottish Rounders Association. *1889.*

First International Cross Country Championships. *1903:* Hamilton.

Canoeing as a modern sport: **John Macgregor** in *1865.*

The oldest tennis court still in use in Great Britain: Falkland Palace.

First rugby international. *1871:* held in Edinburgh. Scotland won.

First football international. *1872:* held in Glasgow. 0-0 draw.

First seven-a-side rugby tournament. *1883:* Melrose.

First skating club. *1778:* Edinburgh.

First golfing tournament. *1774:* Edinburgh.

The world's first 18 hole golf course. *1764:* St. Andrews.

First club badge. *1802:* Duddingston Curling Club.

First women's golf tournament. *1811:* Musselburgh.

First inter-club golf match. *1818:* Edinburgh.

First national sports association. *1838:* Edinburgh.

First professional golf tournament. *1860:* Prestwick.

First municipal bowling green. *1860:* Edinburgh.

Scientific instruments designed by Scots

The reflecting or Gregorian telescope: **James Gregory.** *1638-75.*

The viscometer: **James Hannay.** *1855-1935.*

"Philosopher's beads" to measure the specific gravity of liquids: **Alexander Wilson.** *1714-86.*

The electromagnetic pendulum: **Alexander Bain.** *1810-77.*

The dioptric lens: **Sir David Brewster.** *1781-1868.*

The stereoscope: **Sir David Brewster.** *1781-1868.*

The scintillation counter for measuring radioactivity: **Sir Samuel Curran.** b. *1912.*

The solar reflector: **Thomas Drummond.** *1797-1840.*

The continuous seismograph: **Sir James Ewing.** *1855-1935.*

The live box for studying animals under the microscope: **John Goodsir.** *1814-67.*

The first clock to record split seconds: **James Gregory.** *1638-75.*

Apparatus for the absolute measurement of currents: **Lord Kelvin.** *1824-1907.*

The mirror galvanometer: **Lord Kelvin.** *1824-1907.*

The electric strain gauge: **Lord Kelvin.** *1824-1907.*

The Kerr cell: **John Kerr.**

The achromatic lens: **James Gregory.** *1638-75.*

The siphon recorder: **Lord Kelvin.** *1824-1907.*

The Kelvin ampère balance: **Lord Kelvin.** *1824-1907.*

The electrostatic voltmeter: **Lord Kelvin.** *1824-1927.*

The differential thermometer: **Sir John Leslie.** *1766-1832.*

The hygrometer: **Sir John Leslie.** *1766-1832.*

The photometer: **Sir John Leslie.** *1766-1832.*

Polarising prisms: **William Nichol.** *1768-1851.*

The gravitating compass: **James Sinclair.** *1821-82.*

The ball headed magnet: **John Robison.** *1739-1805.*

The hydrophone: **Robert Stevenson.** *1772-1850.*

The Stevenson screen for thermometers: **Thomas Stevenson.** *1818-1887.*

The microtome: **Archibald Stirling.** *1811-81.*

The prism photometer: **William Swan.** *1818-94.*

The alkalimeter: **Andrew Ure.** *1816.*

The eidograph: **William Wallace.** *1768-1843.*

The bi-metal thermostat: **Andrew Ure.** *1830.*

The chorograph: **William Wallace.** *1768-1843.*

The cloud chamber: **Charles Wilson.** *1869-1959.*

Scottish contribution to agriculture

Test tube baby pigs: **Eddie Straiton.** *b. 1917.*

Kew Botanical Gardens: founded by **Sir William Hooker** in *1841.*

First swedes in Britain: planted by the 18th century inventor **Patrick Miller** *1731-1815,* as a gift to him from the King of Sweden.

The iron milk vessel: an employee of the Shotts Iron Works.

The modern reaping machine: **Patrick Bell.** *1799-1867.*

The application of steam power to agriculture: **William Harley.** *b. 1789.*

The application of chemical principles to agriculture: **Frances Home.** *1719-1813.*

The first commercially successful threshing machine: **Andrew Meikle.** *1719-1811.*

The first threshing machine: **Michael Menzies** in *1732.*

The pulsating milking machine: **Stewart Nicholson.** *1864-1960.*

The winnowing machine: **Andrew Rodger.**

The two-horse swing plough: **James Small** d. *1793.*

The subsoil plough: **James Smith.** *1789-1850.*

Chemical and industrial processes developed by Scots

Distillation of tar: **Archibald Cochrane,** 9th Earl of Dundonald. *1749-1831.*

Manufacture of sal volatile: **James Davie** and **James Hutton.** *1726-1797.*

Caledonian Jade Green, the fastest dye of its time: **Sir James Morton.** *1868-1943.*

Malleable iron using coal rather than charcoal: Carron Iron Works.

Manufacture of caustic soda from salt: **9th Earl of Dundonald.** *1749-1831.*

Manufacture of sal ammoniac by the sublimation of soot: **James Davie** and **James Hutton.** *1726-1797.*

Development of tungsten/vanadium/manganese steels: **Robert Mushet.** *1811-1891.*

The layering system of four colour printing: **John Bartholomew.** *1880.*

The manufacture of writing paper by the chemical bleaching of rags: **Joseph Black.** *1728-99.*

The fan blast for the heating and melting of metals: **James Carmichael.** *1829.*

Water softening: **Thomas Clark.** *1801-67.*

The soap test for determining the hardness of water: **Thomas Clark.**

The use of compressed air in tunnelling: **10th Earl of Dundonald.** *1775-1860.*

Stereotyping in printing: **William Ged.** *1690-1749.*

The use of sulphuric acid as a bleaching agent: **Frances Home.** *1719-1813.*

The use of chlorine for the sterilisation of the water supply: **Sir Alexander Houston.** *1865-1933.*

Extraction of quinine from cinchona: **Sir George King.** *1840-1909.*

Use of albumen as a catalyst in photographic processing: **Lord Kinnaird.**

Effective artificial congelation: **Sir John Leslie.** *1766-1832.*

The use of compressed air to drive machinery: **William Murdoch.** *1754-1839.*

The cyanide process of extracting gold from its ore: **John MacArthur.** *1857-1920.*

The dyes cudbear and Turkey red: **George MacIntosh.** *1739-1807.*

The printer's roller: **Hugh Maxwell.**

The production of gas lighting from coal: **William Murdoch.** *1754-1839.*

Direct process of making steel from bar iron: **David Mushet.** *1772-1847.*

Petroleum oil refining: **James Young.** *1811-83.*

The manufacture of radium compounds: **John Macarthur.** *1857-1920.*

Cast steel: **Robert Mushet.** *1811-91.*

Self hardening tool steel: **Robert Mushet.** *1811-91.*

The hot blast process in furnaces: **James Neilson.** *1792-1865.*

The underground gasification of coal: **Sir William Ramsay.** *1850-1916.*

Nickel steel: **James Riley.** *1889.*

The experimental production of radium from uranium: **Frederick Soddy.** *1877-1956.*

The chenille process of weaving: **James Templeton.** *1839.*

The means of producing a dry, bleaching powder: **Charles Tennant.** *1768-1838.*

The extraction of oil from shale: **James Young.** *1811-83.*

Subjects developed by Scots: "The Fathers"

Applied rheology: **William Scott Blair.** *b. 1902.*

Osmics (the study of odourous substances): **John Kenneth.** *b. 1881.*

Sociology: **Adam Ferguson,** *1724-1816,* the 18th century social philosopher.

Economics: **Adam Smith.** *1723-1790.*

Rational Philosophy: **David Hume.** *1711-1776.*

Mineral optics: **Ernest Anderson.** *1877-1960.*

Neurology: **Sir Charles Bell.** *1774-1842.*

Naval medicine: **Sir Gilbert Blane.** *1749-1834.*

Crystallography: **Sir David Brewster.** *1781-1868.*

Weather forecasting: **Alexander Buchan.** *1827-1907.*

Pharmacology: **Sir Robert Christison.** *1797-1882.*

Chemotherapeutics: **Sir Thomas Fraser.** *1841-1920.*

Experimental geology: **Sir James Hall.** *1761-1832.*

Gynaecology: **William Hunter.** *1718-83.*

Geology: **James Hutton.** *1726-97.*

Experimental optics: **Sir David Brewster.** *1781-1868.*

Antiseptic surgery: **Joseph Lister.** *1827-1912.*

Electronics: **James Clerk Maxwell.** *1831-79.*

Statistical mechanics: **James Clerk Maxwell.** *1831-79.*

Oceanography: **Sir John Murray.** *1841-1914.*

Military medicine: **Sir John Pringle.** *1707-82.*

Naval architecture: **John Scott Russell.** *1808-82.*

Obstetrics: **William Smellie.** *1740-95.*

Mathematical morphology: **Wentworth d'Arcy Thomson.** *1860-1948.*

The Scots as star-gazers

The first magnetic astronomical observatory was set up by **Sir Thomas Brisbane** in *1841* near Kelso.

The first use of kites for meteorological purposes: *1749.* **Alexander Wilson.**

The demonstration that cloud, fog and the colours of the sunset are caused by minute particles of dust in the atmosphere: **John Aitken.** *1839-1919.*

The discovery of the star Nova Aurigae: *1780's.* **T D Anderson.**

The invention of the aplanatic telescope: **Robert Blair.** *1752-1828.*

The connection between sunspots and magnetic storms: **John Brown.** *1817-79.*

The mapping of isotherms and isobars: **Alexander Buchan.** *1827-1907.*

Invention of the sunshine recorder: **John Campbell.** *1822-85.*

Observations of most of the 7,385 stars included in the Brisbane Catalogue of stars of the Southern hemisphere: **James Dunlop.** *1795-1848.*

Elucidation of the nature of aurora borealis: **James Farquharson.** *1781-1843.*

The nebular theory of astronomy: **James Ferguson.** b. *1710.*

The application of scientific principles to the study of glaciers: **James Forbes.** *1809-68.*

The application of photography to astronomical observations: **Sir David Gill.** *1843-1914.*

Discovery of the companion of Antares: **James Grant.** *1788-1865.*

Proposal of the reflecting telescope: **James Gregory.** *1638-75.*

The accurate determination of the stellar and lunar parallax: **Thomas Henderson.** *1798-1844.*

Measurement of the distance of a fixed star: **Thomas Henderson.** *1798-1844.*

Determination of the solar parallax: **James Short.** *1710-68.*

The scientific explanation of the occurrence of dew: **William Wells.** *1757-1817.*

The explanation of sunspots: **Alexander Wilson.** *1714-86.*

Scottish firsts in education

First state secondary schools in the UK.

First state free primary education system in the UK.

The first educational cruise in the UK.

The first cookery class in the UK.

First elementary education system in the UK.

The world's first school for the deaf and dumb.

The first infant school in Britain.

The first technical college in the UK.

First teacher training college in Britain.

First school English department.

First systematic University engineering course.

First University Department of Canadian Studies in the UK.

First international academic seminar linked by satellite.

First teaching laboratory in Britain.

First Chair in Housing Administration.

First free kindergarten.

First University Department of Parapsychology.

The world's first Mechanics Institute.

The world's first technological University.

First systematic training for nurses.

First University to admit women as medical students.

First Chair of Medicine in the UK.

First Chair of Agriculture in the world.

The first correspondence school to prepare candidates for professional examinations.

First Chair of Technical Chemistry in the world.

First Chair of Engineering in the UK.

First Chair of Naval Architecture in the world.

First Students Representative Council in the UK.

First art college in the UK.

First undergraduate course in meteorology.

The first (and only) Department of Artificial Intelligence in Europe.

World's first Chair in Midwifery.

First teaching laboratory for bacteriology in the UK.

First Education Act in Europe to introduce an element of compulsory education.

First marine laboratory in the UK.

The world's first Chair of Anatomy.

The world's first Chair of Materia Medica.

Scientific terms introduced by Scots

Nucleus
Hypnosis
Kinetic
Convergent series
Logarithms
Fixed air
Latent heat
Colloid
Crystalloid
Dialysis
Osmics
Statistics
Hypnotism
Limelight
Atmolysis
Eocene
Potential
Specific heat
Devonian
Antiseptic
Progress
Silurian
Horse power
Cracking

The Scots contribution to banking

Watermarks on bank notes.

The investment trust movement.

The industrial bank.

The first French bank.

The Bank of England.

The Penny Bank.

The first Savings Bank.

Banking on the limited liability principle.

Cash credit: the forerunner of the overdraft.

The principle of banks holding each other's notes in times of monetary stress.

The elaboration of the branch-agency system.

The operation of large scale joint stock banking.

Financial involvement in hire purchase in the UK.

Computer technology in banking in the UK.

Dividend on purchase.

Motor insurance.

Scottish minerals

Brewsterite
Scotlandite
Greenockite
Caledonite
Leadhillite
Allanite
Hopeite
Jamesonite

Scottish firsts and a few lasts

First rubber air bed. *1824: Glasgow.*

First inflatable lifejacket. *1824: Glasgow.*

First major municipal tramway system in the world. *1894: Glasgow.*

First organised group travel excursions. *1841: Glasgow.*

First temperance hotel in Britain. *1861: Edinburgh.*

First naturalist to use the technique of dredging: **Edward Forbes.** *1815-1854.*

First vessel to be sunk in the Second World War: "Athenia", built on the Clyde.

First automobile road fatality. *1834: Paisley.*

First mine in the world to be lit by electricity. *1881: Hamilton.*

Last double decker tram in Great Britain was built for Glasgow Corporation.

First naval dockyard to be built of concrete. *1909: Rosyth.*

First full time public observatory in the UK. *1980: Dundee.*

First scheduled airmail flight in Britain. *1934: Inverness-Kirkwall.*

First aircraft to land on a moving ship. *1917: from Orkney.*

First war correspondent: **William Russell** for The Times during the Crimean War.

The last shot at the Battle of Waterloo: fired by the 71st Highland Light Infantry.

First artificial international language: compiled by **George Dalgarno** in *1651.*

First statistical social survey: **Sir John Sinclair.** *1754-1835.*

The original model for Britannia on the British coinage: a well known Scots beauty at the Court of Charles II.

Edinburgh Zoo was the first to breed King Penguins in the 1920's.
ack: The Royal Zoological Society of Scotland.

First major municipal tramway system in the world. Glasgow.
ack: T and R Annan and Sons Limited, Glasgow.

First sprinkler system for fire prevention. *1881: Edinburgh.*

First shoemakers to introduce rubber heels. *1889: Aberdeen.*

First country motor bus service in the UK. *1897: Hamilton.*

First motor lifeboat. *1909: Orkney.*

First police van or Black Maria. *1911:* supplied to the Glasgow police.

First mobile library van. *1921: Perth.*

First language tuition by radio. *1925: Glasgow.*

First trans Atlantic telephone cable. *1956: Oban-Newfoundland.*

First royal film location. *1896: Balmoral.*

First mobile public toilets. *17th century: Edinburgh.*

First passenger to travel in a steel boat. *1858:* **David Livingstone.**

First television in a public place. London branch of the Caledonian Club.

First woman KC. *1945:* **Margaret Kidd.**

First "keep left" traffic regulations. *1772:* Scottish Act of Parliament.

First Chamber of Commerce in the English speaking world *1783: Glasgow.*

First Boys Brigade Battalion. Founded in *1883.* Glasgow.

First white man to discover the phenomenon of Siamese twins: **Robert Hunter.**

The founder of the YMCA: **David Naismith** of Glasgow.

The founder of the Thames River Police: **Patrick Colquhoun** of Glasgow. *1745-1820.*

First zoo to breed king penguins: Edinburgh Zoo in the *1920s.*

First electric fire alarm system. *1878: Glasgow.*

First railway station to be lit by electricity. *1879: Glasgow.*

First hotel to be lit by electricity. *1881: Glasgow.*

First art gallery to be lit by electricity. *1881: Edinburgh.*

First military campaign medal. *1650:* after the Battle of Dunbar.

Britain's first filtered water supply. *1802: Paisley.*

First steamer to make a sea voyage. *1815: Glasgow-Dublin.*

First Post Office box number. *1830: Edinburgh.*

First ocean sounding in 1840 by **Sir James Ross** *1800-1862.*

The last sea going paddle steamer: the "Waverley", built on the Clyde.

The first white man to cross Australia from South to North: **John McDowell Stuart.** *1815-66.*

The world's first tension leg oil platform: built in Scotland for Conoco's Hutton Field.

The oldest subscription library in Britain. *1741: Leadhills.*

The oldest bell in Europe. *1110:* St. Nicholas Church, Lanark.

The first child to be delivered by anaesthesia. *1847:* **Wilhelmina Carstairs.**

The first cycling offence. *1842:* **Kirkpatrick MacMillan.**

The world's first lady cyclist: *1840's* **Mary Marchbank.**

The world's first floral clock. *1904: Edinburgh.*

The smallest professional theatre in the UK: Mull.

The founder of the Ordnance Survey. **William Roy:** *1726-90.*

The UK's first car manufacturer to achieve volume production. *1900: Glasgow.*

The first envelope known to have been used in Britain was sent by a Scot to a Scot in *1696.*

The first girl guide troop. *1908: Glasgow.*

The first multiple retail shop. *1856:* Singers, Glasgow.

The first dog trained for law enforcement purposes. *1816: Aberdeenshire.*

First temperance societies in the UK. *1828: Greenock and Glasgow.*

First dry cleaner's in the UK 1866 (decorated for a Royal visit in 1914)
ack: Perth Museum and Art Gallery.

An artist's impression of one of Young's refineries at Addiewell, founded in 1866.
ack: BP Oil Grangemouth Refinery Limited.

First person to describe himself professionally as a "Landscape Architect": **Patrick Geddes.** *1854-1932.*

The world's first aerial propaganda raid: **Admiral Thomas Cochrane** *1775-1860* during the Napoleonic Wars.

First person to light his house with gas. *1793:* **William Murdoch.** *1754-1839.*

First dry cleaners in the UK. *1866:* Pullars of Perth.

First practical electric motor in the UK. *1839:* **Thomas Davidson.**

First commercial oil refinery in the world. Bathgate: **James Young.** *1811-83.*

The oldest private firm of shipbuilders in the world still in existence. *1711:* **Scotts of Greenock.**

The world's first and only museum of social work: Glasgow.

The UK's first municipal art collection: Glasgow.

The first non-working member of the Masonic movement. *1600:* **John Boswell.**

The first photograph using a magnesium flash: **Charles Piazzi Smith.** *1819-1900.*

The first recognised Boy Scout Troop. *1908:* Glasgow.

The first cruise. **Arthur Anderson:** a founder of the P & O Shipping Line.

The first person in Britain to dissect an elephant: **Patrick Blair.** *1666-1728.*

The first reference to insulating a conductor: **CM.** *1743.*

The first staff canteen: New Lanark: *1819.*

The first person in the UK to take an X-ray photograph: **Archibald Campbell Swinton.** *1863-1930.*

The first person to reverse a marine engine: **James Watt:** *1736-1819.*

The world's first floral clock, to celebrate tercentenary of Royal College of Physicians of Edinburgh.
ack: James Ritchie and Son (Clockmakers) Limited, Edinburgh.

The last ocean-going paddle steamer the "Waverley".
arriving at Ayr on the Clyde.
ack: Rev Clem Robb.

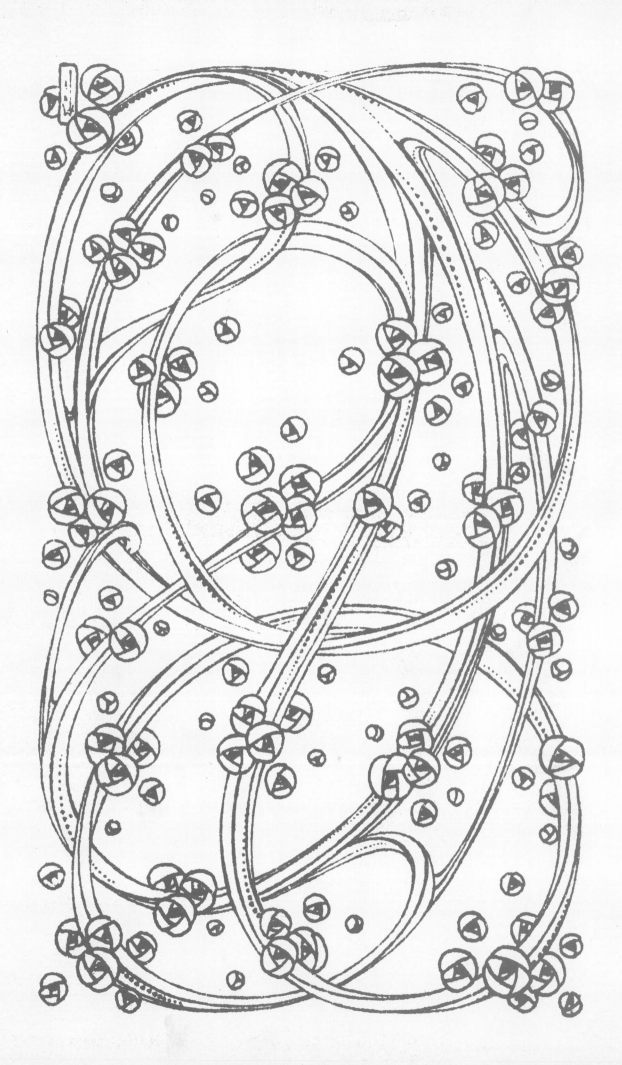